"DO IT AFRAID!"

Bound in the Boat

To One Engineer to Another God has greatness within you!

Rosie,
Dr. Stewart

DR. VALERIE MARTIN-STEWART

All rights reserved. No part of this book may be used or reproduced by any means, graphic, electronics, or mechanical, including photocopying, recording, taping or by any information storage retrieval system without the written permission of the publisher except in the case of brief quotations embodied in critical articles and reviews.

Copyright © 2017 by Dr. Valerie Martin-Stewart

ISBN-13: 978-0-9818152-3-7

ISBN-10: 0-9818152-3-5

Unless otherwise indicated, all scriptures quotations are taken from the King James Version of the Bible.

Dr. Valerie Martin-Stewart

Founder and Executive Director of Taking it by Force Outreach Ministries, Inc.
501 (c)(3) non-profit Ministry

Website: www.takeitbyforce.org
Email: support@takeitbyforce.org

Other Books by Dr. Stewart:

"Out of Pain Came Poetry"
"Rise Above Rejection"
"Miraculous Moments"
"Do it **Afraid!**" Workbook

To book Dr. Stewart for the seminar "**Do It Afraid**" or order her books & products, please visit:

Website: www.valeriemstewart.com
Email: vms@valeriemstewart.com

Printed in the U.S.A.

CONTENTS

ACKNOWLEDGMENTS

INTRODUCTION

CHAPTER ONE: STEPS TO MAXIMIZING YOUR POTENTIAL

CHAPTER TWO: THE MINIs AND MAXIs OF FEAR

CHAPTER THREE: HOW TO FACE FEAR

CHAPTER FOUR: THE PHASES OF FAILURE

CHAPTER FIVE: FAILURE PRODUCES FEAR

CHAPTER SIX: HOW TO OVERCOME FAILURE

CHAPTER SEVEN: CAUSES OF DEPRESSION

CHAPTER EIGHT: DEPRESSION TURNED OUTWARD

CHAPTER NINE: HOW TO OVERCOME DEPRESSION

CHAPTER TEN: HOW TO OVERCOME SHAME

CHAPTER ELEVEN: CAUSES OF SETBACKS IN CAREERS & LIFE

CHAPTER TWELVE: WHAT TO DO IN A SETBACK

CHAPTER THIRTEEN: HOW TO TURN EVERY SETBACK INTO A COMEBACK

CHAPTER FOURTEEN: SOARING HIGH IN YOUR CAREER & LIFE

CHAPTER FIFTEEN: DO "IT" AFRAID!

CONCLUSION

ACKNOWLEDGMENTS

I give thanks to my Savior, Lord and King, Jesus Christ. For it is He and He alone who has saved me and empowered to me live a God-filled and amazing life! It is He who has enabled me to face ALL of my fears and given me the heart and courage to simply "Do It **Afraid!**"

I give special thanks to my gifted and savvy nephew, Jonathan "Quinn" Martin of Texas for all the support by designing my websites, converting my books into Kindle and e-books, sharing your million-dollar techniques and approach; for your unending motivation inspiring me to be more, do more and simply give people the products they're asking for. Forgive me for my slothfulness and fear to accelerate at the speed that you saw and knew I could.

I give thanks to all of you who have attended my seminar entitled "**Do It Afraid!**" since 2007. Many of you have inquired about the book, CDs, and DVDs and I have reluctantly told you none existed. So, today, I am humbled to have been inspired by Quinn and each of your words long enough to sit down and finally write the book.

I give thanks to all of my family, friends and educators (both inside and outside the classroom) for the lessons you've taught me.

INTRODUCTION

I've been blessed to travel many places in the world, for both personal and professional reasons. I've met many people who've shared their goals, dreams and outlook on life. Many have shared with me their desire to go back to school, start a business, travel to some distant place, start a family and others, end a family. Often, I will ask them if they have pursued their goals and they tell me no. I then ask "why" and they tell me, because they *fear failure*. You would not believe just how many times I have heard this!

I'm blown away with just how many people are walking around daily with goals, desires, passions and a longing to experience a fulfilled life, yet they feel trapped and bound by their fears and present circumstances. The number one area that people have shared why they feel so unfulfilled is with their current job. Many people literally dread getting up going to their job, yet due to longevity, the economy, children in college or on their way to college, lack of education, etcetera keep them bound and cause them to become stagnant, complacent and live in their comfort zones.

Yet I truly believe that one hasn't really lived until they live outside of their comfort zone. It requires faith for sure. *I believe a life lived in fear without taking risk is an unfulfilled life*.

I recall being in high school, about the 11th grade. I was walking through my oldest sister's house as a Les Brown VHS played in the VCR. (This generation have no clue what a VHS and VCR is). I cannot tell you what he was *saying*, but my inner man connected with what he was *doing*. I was moved no doubt. I stopped and stared at the television and these thoughts came over me; "I would love to do that one day. I would love to stand before people and say just *one* word to help people move from *where they are* to *where they need to be*. But I resolved within myself that I'd never be able to do this, because I fear public speaking, I care about what everybody thinks of me, I'm shy, I'm timid, I stutter when I talk and people say I talk so slow."

As those thoughts came and went, I soon walked into another room forgetting what I had just desired within, because I felt it was too far-fetched and bottom line, impossible.

So, I'm totally amazed that today, I'm a Motivational and Keynote Speaker doing the very thing I thought was impossible! Many people have called me a "Change Agent." Stating that I have the power and gifting to walk into any room and *increase* productivity and *decrease* absentees. So, I ask you, "What desires do you have or have you had since you were a child, and what's keeping you from fulfilling them?" I hope if fear is keeping you bound, that you will step out of your fears today and simply "Do it **Afraid**!" After having those thoughts, twenty-seven years later I stepped out to pursue my passion of becoming that inspiring speaker. I believe decisions I made within those twenty-seven years pushed and propelled me towards this passion within me. While I haven't made all right decisions from then until now, I believe my wrong choices ultimately led me back to pursuing my destiny.

Often as I'm presenting this seminar entitled "Do it **Afraid**," I always ask how many fear failure and at least 90% of hands *always* go up. The reasons people give are amazing. People have given many reasons, but they always seem to boil down to one common area; they fear trying something, not getting it right and others will know they didn't succeed and therefore, they will be left feeling like a real failure. While conducting one of these seminars I received a revelation and that is, ***the person who tries and fails is not a failure, so as long as s/he gets back up. The real failure is the one who NEVER tries and goes to the grave with dreams, passions and goals locked within that they never pursued all because they were bound by their fears***. Confucius said "Our greatest glory is in never failing, but rising every time we fall."

It was at that awe-struck moment that I became more driven to help others face their fears, as I do the same each and every day. You see, public speaking has always been my number one fear! Yes, can you believe it? I've never taken a speech class in my life as I desperately avoided them; both in high school and in college. Yet today, I'm *doing it afraid* as I stand to preach, teach, and conduct keynote addresses throughout the country.

I will not have done an adequate job of introducing this subject "Do It **Afraid**" if I do not share with you where this all began. In 2007, I was reading my Bible over in Matthew 14: 25-29 where it talks about Jesus walking on the water and how His disciples were afraid that it was a ghost. Jesus simply calms their fears by acknowledging that it was He and to not be afraid.

Peter, one of the disciples, says, "Lord, if it be thou, bid me to come." Jesus simply says, "Come" and Peter steps out of the boat and walks toward Jesus. Yes, for the pessimistic folk, I'm aware that Peter began to sink when he took his eyes off Jesus. And this is exactly what I've heard many ministers focus on when they preach or teach this story. However, I'm optimistic and I was given some profound revelations in this story.

First, the Bible says "They were all afraid" and not they were all afraid, except Peter. So, I believe without a shadow of a doubt, that when Peter stepped out of that boat, all fear had not left him. I believe he still had some underlining fear in his mind about whether he could and would make it to Jesus by walking on the water. Yet, he simply stepped out of the boat and "Did it Afraid."

I also believe that those other eleven disciples were the naysayers as they probably reminded Peter that he is a man, and that Jesus is God's Son and therefore, he wasn't capable of walking on the water as Jesus. I believe they taunted him, casted doubt in him and were the culprits as to why he took his eyes off Jesus and focused on the water, the waves and the roughness of the sea versus the God of all seas. If you'd simply open your spiritual eyes and look around, you'd recognize that you too have many negative people *in your boat* who don't want you to step out and do bigger things, simply because they don't plan to.

Don't allow other people's fears to become your fears! You are destined to succeed, but you *must* leave not just some, but *many* behind!

Secondly, it dawned on me that Jesus had given each of those other disciples the power and the ability to walk on the water also, yet they chose to stay in the boat, their comfort zone. The nails and wood represented their comfort zone, but to walk on liquid (something they were used to drinking and bathing in) was way out of their comfort zone. To use a common resource supply in an uncommon manner was unheard of. They were use to fishing and sailing on the seas. They were use to the wood and the nails beneath them, providing comfort to go from one location to another by boat.

However, never had they walked on the water from one place to another, so for Jesus to tell Peter to come, had to sound absurd and out right foolish to them all. However, we should all want to be wherever Jesus is. If He is in the boat, we should desire to be in the boat, but if He is on the water, we should desire to be on the water as well. Peter desired just that. Too many times we allow the naysayers to prevent us from "stepping out of our boats" to experience something new, live out our passion, do what's never been done, and live a fulfilled life.

Like the wood and nails, we typically find our comfort zone and work, live and play right there. Eventually we die there, in our boring, but comfortable comfort zone. Even though we know there is more to life than what we are experiencing; more to us than what we are producing, we get caught, stuck and therefore settle for the "wood and nails" in our lives. The boat was a hard surface that they sat on and too many times we settle for the hard places in our lives instead of reaching further and stepping out into something greater. *We learn how to function in our dysfunctions*. I truly believe in order for each of us to experience the greatness that life has to offer us, we must be willing to use common resources in uncommon manners. Go for it, today!

Thirdly, Peter is the ONLY man that can ever testify that he walked on the water as Jesus did. What a testimony!!! Whether he walked on the water for five seconds, three seconds or one second. The point is *he walked on the water*! BUT REMEMBER, he wasn't the ONLY one given the power and ability to walk on the water; I believe had they all "got up" and stepped out of the boat and began walking towards Jesus they too would have walked on the water. Furthermore, I believe that when Jesus said, "Come" it was a *universal command* that extended far beyond Peter and the other eleven disciples but to all generations; I believe that command extends to our generation and the generations to come. We're all called to do greater and become more.

Oh, what a failed opportunity for the eleven disciples; but what's even worse are the failed opportunities that you and I let slip right past us daily due to our fears! Peter refused to allow fear, doubt and disbelief keep him bound to the wood and the nails in his current situation. He desired more; he longed for more; *he sensed the greatness that was within him all because of the Greater One who sought the outer him.* Peter knew there was more to life than what he was currently experiencing and he pursued it!!! He went for it, live or die, sink or swim, but he truly "Did it Afraid!"

So, this is where my title "Do It **Afraid**" was derived from. I desire not to be like one of the eleven disciples who had the power to do the same as Peter did, yet they let their fears keep them bound in the boat! How many of you reading this book today are letting your fears keep you bound and shackled to your boat and staying in your comfort zone; even though you've been given power to help you accomplish and achieve everything that you put your hands to? How long will you continue to sit there in your comfort zone?

Take it from me, *never allow yourself to become comfortable in an uncomfortable situation.* I believe this is the root cause why so many people are living such a dreadful and unfulfilled life. You are not happy in your current condition, however, because it's a place of comfort, you have conditioned and psyched yourself into believing you are doing good. **You have mastered managing your dysfunctions**.

Too often we settle for whatever hand life deals us and we try to compensate, improvise and you name it just to cope. However, stop coping with any and everything in your life that you're not happy about! You and I possess the power and ability to change our current circumstances, but we must be willing and simply "get out of the boat."

I'm determined to empower everyone I encounter to never settle for less; never stay in your comfort zone; experience life by exposing yourself to life; and to simply "Do it **Afraid**!" If you are in your comfort zone, then you are perhaps like the man who was in jail. His bail was paid and the bars were open wide for him to walk out a free man, yet he continued to sit in the jail cell. He had become very comfortable in that cell and fear gripped him to walk outside of the little space he had become accustomed to. *Why are you still sitting there?*

Sigmund Freud said, "Most people do not really want freedom because freedom involves responsibility and most people are frightened of responsibility."

Perhaps you're like the young eagles that took a class to learn how to fly. After sitting in class for six months and having gain all the knowledge, skills and tools to be able to fly, the last day of class they *walked* out. Did you catch it? They should have flown out, but instead they walked out. Why?

[They failed to apply what they had heard and learned those six months. *We must apply what we learn.*]

At the end of many of my seminars I tell the people, you can buy all the books, CDs, DVDs, etc. and listen to them day and night. But until you *implement* what you've read or heard, none of this will be effective in your life or produce any good fruit.

CHAPTER ONE

STEPS TO MAXIMIZING YOUR POTENTIAL

• STEP OUT OF FEAR

Believe in yourself - You must know that if you are going to truly maximize your potential you must believe in yourself 100% and 100% of the time. You can't allow doubt to creep in your mind due to your past failures or through other's words of doubt to you.

Your belief must be that you can and will achieve all that you were created to achieve before you leave this earth. You can't allow your present, past, or future fears of whatever keep you in your boat! Start taking steps toward your goal, but remember, in doing so, like Peter, you must leave many behind. Move anyway, for like the four leprous men in 2nd King 7:3, **you will die if you stay where you are**.

• STEP OUT OF FAILURE

Get up Again with Purpose - You must realize that we all have failed in life at one thing or another. All of us have strengths and weaknesses. We will not succeed in everything. However, you don't have to stay there. As I stated earlier, as long as you get back up again, then you are not considered a failure.

The real failure is the one who never tries and goes to the grave with passions, dreams and goals locked inside.

So, get up, don't stay down. Once you are up, take inventory of yourself, of why you failed in the first place. Was it the wrong thing to pursue, was it the wrong people working along side you or did you allow past failures to impact your current pursuit?

To experience success, you must be willing to evaluate and take an honest look at why you failed. Whatever negativity you discover, remove them. Don't allow negative people, your own negative thoughts or past failures have any influence on your destination for the future. You were born to succeed and win in the very thing that brings you joy and comes natural for you!

- **STEP OUT OF DEPRESSION**

Rise and determine to move forward – While working on my doctorate some years ago, I discovered that I had been depressed most of my life (both childhood and adult life). Interesting enough, I discovered most people experience depression on a daily and sometimes weekly basis. Some due to losing a job, others due to losing a pet, a loved one, and the list goes on. We experience many losses throughout our lives that could bring on depression. However, like failures, the key is not to stay depressed. The key is to recognize the symptoms and seek help.

Depression will come and go, but it can only last if you allow it. Some have experienced chronic depression as I have, but the key is, I didn't stay there. Depression is a robber of the soul. It will eat at you mentally, spiritually, emotionally and even physically. Depression is the onset of many health problems that people experience daily. However, many have no clue that they are depressed, because they have felt that way for years and have learned how to cope and function in that low mental state.

Depression doesn't look like it did years ago. Many remain very functional attending to their spouses, children, chores, jobs, etc. They feel "out of it" most of the time. However, you must rise and not let it get the best of you.

Since starting this book, I will share a most recent time that I slipped into depression and that was when my oldest brother Gene passed and my only child, Paris, went off to college just three months later. I was asked to eulogize my brother's funeral by my nephew, but with all of my seminary training, it did not prepare me to preach at that moment. This was very difficult as well as uncomfortable for me to do, but due to the love for my nephew, I wanted to oblige. To mentally prepare a message, I had to separate myself *internally* with the thought that this wasn't family. However, soon as I finished and as we exited the church, I broke down at the last pew as I heard this, "You just preached your brother's funeral." But I regrouped and committed his body to the grave at the cemetery.

Then three months later, my daughter chose to attend college ten hours away from home at Spelman College in Atlanta, GA. I didn't dare want her to go so far from home. After all, she had been accepted into Old Dominion, George Mason, Hampton University and other universities right in Virginia. Yet my desire to let her spread her wings, follow her dreams and live a fulfilled life, I permitted her to go even though inside, I wanted her to attend somewhere closer.

Meanwhile, I began to slip into depression *unaware*. I found myself having no desire to go to the gym any longer since she and I used to go together. All I was doing was going to work, church and home. By February of the following year, I heard a still small voice say, "You're depressed." I was shocked and began to consider why. And that's when I realized I had not one, but two major losses in my life: the loss of my brother and the seemingly loss of my daughter since she moved so far away. I immediately knew I had to get up and get back in the gym and avoid isolating myself from others.

So, be warned that you and I can easily slip into depression and not even be aware that we are depressed. However, once we realize it, we must seek help immediately if we find ourselves not able to bounce back to some form of normalcy. Know that depression will come and go, but again, the key is not to stay there. Recognize the signs and seek help immediately.

• STEP OUT OF SHAME
You have something unique to offer - By now you may see that fear breeds failure, and failure breeds depression. Depression breeds shame and many other things. Every time we fail at something in life, especially if others know of our failures, we tend to feel embarrassment and shame. However, you can't sit in shame if you plan to maximize your full potential. You must know that shame is only temporary. We all feel shame, but you have the power to reverse shame.

Don't sit and wallow in your shame. You must recognize the uniqueness of your gifts and talents and step out of it. There are things that you do very well with no struggle at all. There are problems you are able to resolve without much effort of your own. As you recognize the uniqueness of your gifts, pursue them. Don't become a victim of your shame. Shame was never meant to be worn by those who are gifted, creative, and born to win.

• STEP OUT OF SETBACKS
Discover the passions within - If you are truly going to take every *setback* and turn them into a *comeback,* you must discover your own passions. What is it that you shine in? What brings you great joy? What comes natural to you? What job would you pursue and be excited about getting up to go to everyday if you were already a millionaire and all your bills were paid? What would you do for free? Nine times out of ten, that is where your passion lies.

I love speaking and empowering others! Yet public speaking is *still* my #1 fear!!! I have done a lot of Keynote Addresses pro bono! Yes, I said, for free. Some of these venues have been at large government agencies in the Washington, D.C. area. Many have asked me why and I simply tell them, because I love it! I truly don't believe anyone could pay me the right amount of money to equate to the joy it brings me to speak. Now if someone tried, I would not object. So, find out what motivates and excites you! Then pursue it and if you can get paid while doing it, life will be even sweeter. Everyone have at least one passion, some have more. Discover yours and work it.

CHAPTER TWO

THE MINIs and MAXIs OF FEAR

FEAR CAUSES US TO:

- **MINIMIZE OUR VIEW & VALUE OF SELF** - It's true, I'm my own worst critic. I believe that most people are their worst critic as well. Being your own worst critic is not necessarily a bad thing. What's bad about it is when you fail to realize how valuable you are in every setting you find yourself. You see, you bring to the table what others don't. They may desire to, but they are not gifted in the same area that you are.

- You have valuable knowledge, wisdom, life-lessons, understanding, and know-how about certain things in life. Your ability to step into a room, a business meeting, family gathering, etc. and change the entire atmosphere is incomparable. You possess talents, gifts and passions that automatically stir up the gifts in others. However, you must realize it. If you are not careful, your fears will cause your view and value of yourself to be distorted

- You must never allow fear to minimize the great value you have to offer. Your *presence* adds volumes to any environment.

- **MAXIMIZE** OTHER'S VALUE - Just as fear causes you to overlook and never see your own value, meanwhile, it causes you to value other's greater than yourself. This is definitely an untruth. While others do bring value to the table, it's so important that you don't allow yourself to believe what they have to offer is more important than what you have to offer.

- Imagine your body, the head, even though it's great, it can never say to the eyes, legs, or heart that I don't need you. Likewise, the liver, lungs, and kidneys are quite important, being part of our major organs in our bodies, but it would be foolish for either of them to think they don't need the blood or any other vital part of the body to function properly.

- Once, I felt that I was unimportant to a group of people and I got this revelation. Even if I'm just a little finger or little toe to that body, if either of them are cut off and the body is not tended to, the entire body can hemorrhage to death. Wow! What a revelation. So, know that while others have gifts, talents and abilities, their gifts are not more important than your own.

- **MINIMIZE** OUR POTENTIAL - Know that you have awesome potential and many times, it's lying dormant. However, due to your fears, you have bought into the lie that where you are today is as far as you can go. Fear blinds, steals, and lie to your psyche telling you that you have achieved all that you can or suppose to achieve in life. That's a lie! Greatness is living inside of you! You must tap into it and realize there are unborn dreams in you that need to be birthed.

- Yes, men too have many dreams and goals inside that need to be birthed. Examples of men who gave birth, Wright brothers birthed the airplane, Bill Gates birthed Microsoft, Steve Jobs birthed Apple products, Bill Cosby birthed the Cosby Show, Dr. Julius Irving and Michael Jordan birthed flying in basketball, Magic Johnson birthed the no-look pass, and there's more.

- So understand that birthing is not merely a physical presence or position, but it's having the right posture (mindset) to achieve and do what's never been done or do it one hundred times better. You see, I don't want to be like anybody. I may work the same craft or share the same brand as another, but I believe I have the potential to take whatever I'm gifted and been called to do to a whole new plateau. I believe you too have the same ability.

- Too often, we compare ourselves to others, believing the level that they have performed at is the maximum level. I beg to differ. There are new medicines, new technologies, new inventions and more that are waiting to be discovered.

Will you be the one to do so? Just like the iPhone or Android phone you now possess, if you are like me, you don't know how to use all the functions that the phone was created for, right? Such a small computer with unending capability right in the palm of our hands. Well...the same is true with you. You have untouched and untapped potential that is waiting to be discovered. Guess who must discover it and then release it? You, so what are you waiting for?

- **MAXIMIZE** THE FEAR OF CHANGE
We all tend to fear change. In my twenty-five plus years of working for the Department of Defense, one thing I've had to get accustomed to is change. Just as soon as I learn how to use our travel system and remembered my password, the system changes. As soon as I got accustomed to one badge, they issued a new one. I'm accustomed to change; do I always like it, no. However, it's inevitable. Change is taking place daily all around us. Especially in the area of technology. We've gone from big clunky computers to small flat screens and touch screens at that. We've gone from big televisions to high definition, smart televisions, flat screens that we can now place on our walls.

- Change is necessary if there will be growth. *A sign God is preparing to bless you abundantly...is when you have to change your physical location.* New seasons bring new people in your life. Others are connected to you achieving your destiny.

You must leave some and be introduced to others. You have gone as far as you were suppose to with them. So, don't fight nor dread change.

- **MINIMIZE** OUR VALUE ADDED - You are born to succeed. You have everything inside of you that is needed to take you to the next level, gain you the next promotion, start your own business, and finish everything you started. However, if you always believe what you have to offer is insignificant while other's value added is greater, you will never reach your plateau in life. Know that your value is the same or greater than all other's value, but you have something different to offer.

- **MAXIMIZE** OUR DISAPPOINTMENTS – We've all experienced disappointments in life. Many of them have come from relationships we found ourselves in. Some have been disappointed on the job, in marriages, with siblings, with father or mother and the list goes on. However, if you plan to move forward and not stop here you must suck it up, pull yourself up by the shoelace and keep moving.

- As long as we live, there will be times where we are entering storms, find ourselves right in the middle of storms or exiting the storms.

- So, the question in life is not if or whether we'll ever experience storms, but simply how to keep advancing and going forward in spite of the storms. Know that storms will come, but no storm last forever. It may rain many days and weeks straight, but eventually, the sun shines again. When it does, it's bigger and brighter. So, know your storms in the form of disappointments can't last forever. Be prepared to rise.

- **MINIMIZE** OUR COMPETENCE – We all tend to feel incompetent in our lives at given moments. Many times what we fail to realize is, that we typically feel this way in areas of our weaknesses. Especially when we compare our weakness to another who is strong in this area.

- What we must realize is that we all have strengths and weaknesses. Find out what you are good in and can do with little to no effort at all, and then work it well. For those areas you don't feel so strong in, simply acknowledge that those are not your strengths. Too many times we allow ourselves to get voted and nominated into positions in both our personal and professional lives in areas we *know we aren't* competent in.

- Then when we take on these positions anyway, sooner or later, our incompetence begins to show. However, we could have avoided this altogether had we been honest in the first place and simply acknowledged that I'm not the right fit for that position, but thanks for the recommendation. Know that you are very competent in some area of your life, but you must be willing to acknowledge both the competent and incompetent areas in order for you to shine bright!

- **MAXIMIZE** OUR WEAKNESSES – We tend to focus on our weaknesses far too many times instead of focusing on our strengths. Understand that your weaknesses are simply a sign that you are human and won't do everything well. While I've heard many say we must work on our weaknesses until they become strengths, I beg to differ. For me, to simply *acknowledge* that I'm not good in this area is really overcoming that weak area.

- Point and case, I once told management that I wanted to be a program manager over a particular program. So, they gave me a chance at becoming one and I had to attend these software meetings. Well...after attending two meetings, it was very clear to me, this was not my expertise neither an area I wanted to serve as program manager. Instead of faking it, as many do, I went to the current program manager and acknowledged to her that software was a weakness of mine and that this is why I changed my major in college from computer science to electrical engineering.

- Management totally understood and thanked me for my honesty. Whew! I was relieved from having to attend those boring meetings and I've now found a job that I'm totally satisfied in.

- Acknowledgment is critical to overcoming any weakness. You will be the better for it and people will respect you greater for your honesty.

CHAPTER THREE

HOW TO FACE FEAR

ACKNOWLEDGE ONE'S WEAKNESS – If you are going to face any and all of your fears, you *must* acknowledge your weaknesses! It's not a question if you will, but when will you. Your weaknesses are not the end of you. Really, they are the beginning of bringing out the best in you! Once your weaknesses are acknowledged, who you are in the form of your strengths will overshadow and outweigh all weaknesses. Then the real you will be manifested and shine brighter!

MAXIMIZE ONE'S STRENGTHS – Now that you have acknowledged your weaknesses, it's now time to showcase your strengths. Know that you were born to perform and fly at great heights. You are an eagle and eagles fly high and have very keen vision. Pilots attested to having seen eagles flying at fifteen thousand feet and higher. So, work your strengths. Don't continue to hang out with barnyard chickens, buzzards, and crows when your eagle nature is calling you to great heights. Some of these birds have an appetite for anything, but your eagle appetite only calls for the best. Know that in working your strengths, you perhaps will outshine leaders and upper management in both your personal and professional life, but realize, that's their problem, not yours. Work your strengths!

STOP SHRINKING! - Too many people shrink in life when they should be thriving in life. I'm guilty, as I've shrunk in the classroom, church and on the basketball court. There were times I knew all the answers for a test or could have easily scored twenty points in games, but I didn't, because I didn't want to outshine my peers around me. I've shrunk in many settings trying to pretend that I didn't know answers in church, seminary, and so forth, but it's no place to live for eagles.

Don't you realize when you shrink in life in any setting you don't enhance other's abilities to shine brighter? You have simply kept others from growing and glowing from you and all that you have to offer. As author, lecturer, congressional hopeful Marianne Williamson has said, "Your playing small doesn't serve the world. There's nothing enlightening about shrinking so that others around you will not feel insecure."

Stop shrinking trying to make others feel comfortable, but challenge them to come and fly high where you now fly and meet them in the skies.

LET GO OF PAST FAILURES – All of us have failed in life: in sports, in relationships, in careers, in school, and in our emotions of how we responded poorly in circumstances and situations.

However, in order for you to face your fears, you must understand that your failure is only temporary. Don't you realize some of the most successful people in the world are those who have failed the most?

Consider Abraham Lincoln, Walt Disney, Michael Jordan, Babe Ruth, Oprah, Lucille Ball, and Sidney Poitier. They all experienced great and multiple failures in life, yet each of them got back up again! They didn't stay there! They didn't sit, wallow, and pout in the midst of their failures. Each of them rose to become an all star and world renown in their own perspective crafts! Don't allow your failures to define you for they are not who you are. Sometimes failures steer us in the right direction of what we should be pursuing and sometimes failures serves as a launching pad to catapult us to our perspective destinies!

Point and case: I recall I once worked at a sandwich shop and I was great making sandwiches as long as it wasn't lunchtime. But as soon as lunchtime arrived, I became full of anxiety and rushed to make sandwiches. I made many errors during this time so I felt I would soon be let go of, okay fired. I hate that word.

The little sweet Caucasian lady/owner called me to the side one day and I dreaded what I already knew...I was about to be fired. She told me she loved my sweet spirit, I was cute, and that I would do great things in life one day, but she had to let me go as a sandwich maker because I couldn't handle rush hour. Even though I knew it was coming, I was devastated. I loved making sandwiches at that shop. Meanwhile, my Mom and siblings were telling me to get back in school and finish my degree in engineering. By losing my job as a sandwich maker, I chose to get back in school. I believe had I never lost my job, I might still be there making sandwiches to this day. Realize that sometimes a closed door is only a messenger to steer you back on the path in life you're suppose to be on.

BUILD NEW RELATIONSHIPS – If you are planning to have a major impact on the world, you must be willing and open to welcoming new relationships. Too many times we get stuck with people who are not going anywhere in life and they don't want to see us excel in life either. Some of these people are family, friends, and even coworkers.

However, you must know like Kenny Rogers said in one of his song, "Know when to hold them, know when to fold them, know when to walk away and know when to run." Be open to build and cultivate newfound relationships; particularly with those who are positive, on fire, and seeking to make a difference in the world for the better.

DON'T FEAR SUCCESS! - While most people fear failure, there are a few people in the world who fear success; and some fear a little of them both. I have always feared success.

I've had opportunities to try out and play in the Women's National Basketball Association (WNBA), but my fear of success and what would become of my two year old daughter at that time haunted me deeply. I feared I wouldn't be able to handle the money, the fame, the glamour and much more. I didn't want to draw *friendly enemies*.

The fear of reaching a certain plateau and maintaining that level has always haunted me. So, I chose to stay where I was, working an engineering job that brought little fulfillment in my life. I have often asked this question in my seminar of how many people fear success and a few hands always arise. Many people give the same reasons that I've stated above. However, you must know, if you are going to face every fear and allow God to get the best out of you, you must let go of your fear of success today!

"KNOW THAT COURAGE IS NOT THE ABSENCE OF FEAR, BUT ACTING IN THE VERY MIDST OF IT"

CHAPTER FOUR

THE PHASES OF FAILURE

BECOME ISOLATED – Whenever we experience or feel like a failure in our lives, it automatically causes us to isolate ourselves from others. We begin to believe we are the only ones going through this particular event or change in our lives. We find ourselves talking with defeat, thinking, acting and perhaps praying with an already defeated mindset.

Isolation is not productive for anyone. Isolation only causes us to dwell on our situations and travel further down a road of despair and disbelief. I've failed in many things in life and I've had my share of pity parties. What I noticed in those parties was that, I typically had many who stayed in contact with me desiring to hear how sadder I was the next day. They had no real interest in helping me to arise and get over or come out of the party. They only wanted to verify that I was still there so that they could share with others.

I also noticed that once I began to rise and come out of the party, their phone calls became few to none. Understand that sometimes, it's good to be alone and meditate to gain control and a sense of balance of who we are, the trials we've overcome and the hills we must climb. However, it's never good to be alone due to your failures.

DOUBT SELF-WORTH – Whenever we fail in life, we always believe we are the cause. We used to say on the basketball court, "my bad" whenever we made a mistake. But we must realize that every mistake that happens to us or against us is not always our bad or fault. If we are not careful, we find ourselves believing we are the cause and we doubt our competence. However, you must know that you have something very unique to offer and that your gifts, talents and abilities are needed. Know that there are no duplicates of you, only imitators. Only you can be the best at being you.

BELIEVE WE ARE THE CAUSE – Every time you failed in life, you may have contributed to the failure, but typically, others are at fault as well. I can testify to many failed relationships that I've encountered, I left feeling I was to blame for everything bad that happened.

However, time and wisdom have taught me that while I was at fault in some areas, but the other person involved also did or said some things wrong as well that contributed to the breakdown of the relationship. All too often, we don't like admitting our faults to others, because we feel that it shows weakness on our behalf. But in order for you to heal, you must realize all parties, typically, are at fault, whether they ever admit it or not.

FORGET THE SUCCESSES – Many of us have experienced great successes in our personal and professional lives, but way too often, we forget them and zoom in on the failures or negative things. Just as I played professional basketball in Peru, Australia, and toured in Italy, I seldom talk about those times, because I was living outside of God's will for my life.

I was running from Him and the call to preach on my life. So, when many hear or read about this time in my life and think how awesome it was and desire to hear more, I tend to shy away from the topic. While the outward experience was great, my inner man was as weary as one could be. I was living and working in Australia, the land Down Under, a much desired tourist destination for many, but I was absolutely miserable. I felt as though I was on the dusty roads of Mississippi due to my inner weariness. Therefore, I often forget this time of my life in other countries and rarely do I talk of it. I only bring it up now to use as an example. I am living proof that you can be living in Canaan, but unable to enjoy Canaan when you're not balanced.

INTERNALIZE EVERYTHING – Wow! This has been me all of my life. Every time I failed in some area of my life or experienced hurt, I internalized it. Not only did I internalize it, the thoughts were a constant rewind and play in my mind. I have examined and taken great inventory of myself many of times believing all failures in my life were due to my own actions.

...ne to realize that some of the hurt, and letdowns have been at the ... Perhaps their own inferiorities and ... to appear strong caused me to ...e hurt and accept that all was my fault. ... not suppress what's deep inside of us. We ...st allow it to come to the surface, deal with it for what it is and then move forward.

BECOME LESS DRIVEN – Every time we fail in life, it tends to burst our bubble and take some of the wind out of our sail. Too many people lose hope, drive, and the guts to excel no matter the cost. ***Too often we accept lifelong solutions for some things that were only meant to be temporary.*** You cannot afford to lose your drive for success and reaching your goals in life simply because you've experienced failure.

Whenever you become less driven, others can feel that negative energy and will typical avoid you. You must always surround yourself with people, things and ideas that motivate and inspire you to want to do more daily. Never succumb to the feelings of a loser's attitude. Know that if you plan to fulfill you destiny, you must wake up everyday with a drive and determination that says, "I'm unstoppable." Press forward!

ABANDON OUR GOALS – Not only do we become less driven, but also we altogether forsake or abandon our goals. Never should you allow past failures to cause you to put aside or down your goals. Where there is no vision, the people perish so says the scriptures. You must always set goals, near and long term having a backup plan in place. You will never reach your destiny if you forsake what's inside of you. Many need what you have inside of you. Do what you must, but don't stop here.

CHAPTER FIVE

FAILURE PRODUCES FEAR

WE FEAR FAILURE WHICH KEEPS US FROM TREADING NEW PATHS

Every time you and I fail in life, there is something inside of us that tells us we were not cut out for this and to give up. However, you must know, a give-up attitude is not who you were created to be and exemplify. I don't care how many times you've failed; you must get back up and be willing to try it again.

If you discover in the process that the things you are pursuing are not meant for you, fine. Then try something else. Don't just give up altogether. *Don't allow failure to be the end of you.* Ralph Waldo Emerson said it this way, "Do not travel where the path may lead; instead, travel where there is no path and leave a trail."

Sometimes, even in multiple failures in the same thing, you must keep trying again if you know this is what you are to be pursuing. This was the case with Thomas Edison. It is said that he tried over 1000 times to invent the light bulb and electricity but failed. When reporters asked him how does it feel to have failed 1000 times, he politely replied, "I did not fail 1000 times; I created 1000 steps to the invention of the light bulb." Bam! What a response! So, you see, it's not how others view your failures, but how you view your failures. Now what will you do with your failures?

WE FEAR NEVER GETTING IT RIGHT

Every time we fail, we fear that we will never get it right ever again. But this wasn't the case with Babe Ruth. For most people know he became famous for having hit the most home runs in baseball. But what many failed to realize is that for decades, he also held the record for the most strikeouts as well. He hit 714 home runs and struck out 1330 times in his career. Babe said, "Every strike brought him closer and closer to his next home run." What have you struck out in doing many, many times? How many times have your struck out? Don't you realize you are closer to smashing a home run in your endeavor? You can't quit now! Destiny is calling you! John Wooden once said, "Winners make the most errors." Rightfully so, I would think simply because they are the ones who are constantly trying, failing and getting back up again.

FAILURE BIRTHS GREATER FEAR THAT MAKES US FEEL INCOMPETENT

Too many times we fail in life and when we do, we become even more afraid. We tend to allow one or two failures in our lives sum up our entire life as nothing. Sure, you failed at some things, but you haven't failed at all things. Would you believe that Walt Disney, whose descendants now rake in billions, wasn't always a success? He was fired by a newspaper editor stating, "He lacked imagination." He tried presenting Mickey Mouse to the city of Anaheim, only for them to tell him to get away from them with such an idea and that he would only draw a lot of riffraff. I tell people in my seminars, I would love to be drawing some of the riffraff (money) that Walt's descendants are drawing today. He started businesses only to end in bankruptcy. However, Disney eventually found a recipe for success that worked for him and millions.

Another man who failed yet got back up again was Henry Ford. He is known today for his innovative assembly line and American-made cars, but he didn't start out this way. Early in his career, he started many businesses that failed and left him broke at least five times. However, he is now known for the successful Ford Motor Company.

Confucius said, "Our greatest glory is not in never failing but in rising every time we fall."

Did you know R.H. Macy failed seven times before his store (Macy's) caught on in New York City?

Carl Lewis competed for almost twenty years. When asked of him what did he attribute to his longevity, he said, "Remembering that you have both wins and losses along the way. I don't take either one too seriously."

Did you know Sidney Poitier, at his first audition, was asked by the casting director, "Why are you wasting our time; just go and be a dishwasher or something?" It was at that moment, Poitier recalls, that he decided to devote his life to acting. And the rest is history!

Oprah was told in her early years, that she wasn't "fit" for television. Hmmm, didn't Oprah retire from twenty-five years of hosting "The Oprah Show" and now owns her own network, Oprah Winfrey Network (OWN)? I'm just saying...

I recall having had the opportunity to try out for the WNBA during its inaugural season in 1997. I had done my research, sent out information and stats on myself to each of the team's coaches and I was invited to the Los Angeles Spark's tryout. I was amazed! I told my coworkers and they immediately began to back me up. They helped me watch my eating habits and encouraged me to work out twice a day. I found myself running at lunch time and then again in the evenings after work.

I recall telling one of my brothers about my plans to try out just to get his thoughts. He told me that I needed to forget about basketball since I had already played professionally overseas. He went on to tell me that I had a good engineering job, I'm going through a divorce and I needed to focus on raising my daughter. I was surprised that he wasn't excited about my opportunity; therefore, I succumbed to what he thought I should have been focusing on.

I later told my supervisor my plans as I asked about taking leave of absence from work if/once I made the team. He assured me I could do just that and they would hold my job for me for one year. However, right as I was leaving his office he asked me if I was sure that I could still play with those young girls. (His word casted more doubt as my brother's word already had)

He went on to tell me that I'm older now and most of these girls were fresh out of college with young legs. (I was thirty then and my game had improved tremendously simply because I believed in myself and abilities). I nodded and assured him I could still play with them, but inwardly, I walked away beginning to doubt if I really could.

*It amazes me how often we allow other people's opinions of us **outweigh** our own opinions and actual facts.*

Yet my coworkers continued to support me in ways I found incredible! So, I continued working out with the goal of playing professional sports again, this time in the U.S.A. However, I want you to know, once I showed up in Los Angeles, *fear* gripped me!!! I began to hear things in my head like, your daughter is going to end up on drugs like many star's kids all because you won't have time to raise her as she will be left with others. I did not want to even fathom the thought of her ending up on drugs even though she was only two years old.

I also began to hear my brother and supervisor's words. I let their words of doubt overpower my coworker's words of faith. So, when my feet hit the floor to play, basketball was the very last thing on my mind. I was in the absolute best shape of my life, better than when I played professionally overseas, yet my mind was saturated with fear. *I was prepared physically, but mentally, I was a mess*! Physically I couldn't be denied but mentally I was already defeated. If we are going to succeed in anything in life, *we must get our mouth and our mind in alignment*! Too often we speak one thing and demonstrate something else or vice versa.

The fear was so strong and so overpowering that I couldn't focus on basketball. I knew I could compete with those ladies, as some of them were older than me, yet mentally, I was not there. I couldn't concentrate long enough on basketball to play my game. Foolishly, I went to the board to see if I made the first cut a few hours later. Yet, I did not.

I was sad, feeling rejected, depression, and shame. The shame came from the thought I was going to have to return home and tell my coworkers that I didn't make it. I returned and told them, but I never shared that I *intentionally* played my worse basketball due to fear, fear, and more fear. I also valued my brother and supervisor's words over my very own. What a shame and a missed opportunity.

That failure birthed greater fear and I found myself sinking deeper into shame.

However, that wasn't the end of the story. The Orlando Miracles soon started a team and I received not one but two invitations to go and try out. They sought me out without me ever sending any information on myself. Their letters stated they had heard about me and were thanking me for the tapes I had sent. What? What were they talking about, because I never sent them tapes or anything else? However, I shared this news with my coworkers and they just knew this was God giving me another chance to play in the WNBA. I thought so too, but my fears caused me to not go try out. Ironically, I received the letters in early spring and passed them up.

However, I went to Orlando that same year for Christmas to be with family and I went to a TJ Maxx. Well...guess who was in this store? The coach from Orlando Miracles!!! Our eyes met, and we looked away and we then turned and looked back at each other quickly thinking we knew each other I suppose. I recognized her from the website and thought, that's Coach Carolyn Peck, former coach at Purdue!!! The letters had come from her.

Yet, I was too afraid to approach her thinking by now, they have their team locked in stone. I went home to share with another brother and family of just seeing her. He, being sure I had introduced myself and told her I would be there for the week, went on to tell me I could use their car to go to the tryouts. I had to break the news that I never approached her. He was totally shocked! He began to tell me how big Orlando was and that the chances of me meeting her in a TJ Maxx would be slim to none knowing how many of those stores are there. I began to shrink inside and feel like a bigger loser than I was already feeling. He scorned me for not capitalizing on such a grand opportunity to showcase my talents to her in person during that week.

I just sucked it up and told him I never approached her. When he asked why, I was too ashamed to tell him it was fear. I simply told him I've played pro once so I'm good, but I now was repeating another brother's words spoken to me. That's not how I felt at all! I look back now and see how I've missed so many great opportunities all due to fear overpowering my mind. I *will* capitalize on every opportunity and if I fail, so be it, but *I won't fear fear* or success ever again.

Another perceived failure or setback in my life that has haunted me since a child and that is my speech. People have joked me about my speech since a child saying I talk so slow. So, I learned silence and began to write. However, when I was hosting a spiritual conference in my hometown a few years ago, I had the opportunity to be interviewed on the radio for an hour. As the owner's wife interviewed me he was doing business with another gentleman out front. Once the interview was over, the male owner came over to me and desired to tell me something.

He said, "Understand this, I am a man and love being a man, but **if** I was a woman, I would want your voice, because you have a certain sound that is captivating. So, captivating and moving that I couldn't help but listen in to you even though I had a customer out front." He went on to tell me I was only to be interviewed for 15-20 minutes, but due to my distinct voice, he motioned for his wife (as my back was to the window) to continue on with the interview. So, the 15 minutes interview turned into one hour.

Wow! What? He loved my voice, the one that people have joked me about for years? Well, after thanking them for the opportunity to be on air, I walked to my car deeply puzzled, wondering what in the world did he like about my voice. As I got into my car, I heard this, "***The area that we've been teased the most in life is the area that God desires to use for His glory.***" So, what area have you been made fun of all or most of your life? That area is perhaps your greatest gift!

I was told by friends and relatives that the Canton Spirituals and Lee Williams along with the William brothers return to MS and they're only interviewed for 15 minutes yet I was given an hour. Wow! Really? The voice I grew up hating because others made fun of it, was THIS DAY, a well-received one. Unbelievable unto me for sure!

These are but a few examples that I've chosen to highlight to bring to the forefront of your mind. I ask you now, are you still determined to quit and allow your past failures to define who you are? I didn't think so. Get up, go forward and fly!

CHAPTER SIX

HOW TO OVERCOME FAILURE

ACCEPT DEFEAT FOR THAT MOMENT – You must know that even though you haven't always experienced success in every area of your life, it's only temporary! Yes, you loss; face it, deal with it and move on. One or even a few bad losses in your life don't sum up your entire life or your future. Greater purpose and destiny are inside of you waiting to be tapped into and released.

I've lost games on many teams that I've played basketball with, but we didn't return to our home and hang up our jerseys to never step foot on the court again. No, we went back, practiced the next day, planned, strategized and worked on beating our next opponent.

We never allowed one, two or several losses sum up our entire year as a loss. We kept practicing and performing until the end of season. Then when playoff time came, we had our minds set and our hearts focused on the ultimate goal, to win a championship. Our past losses had no bearing on our present state. You are in the game called 'life;' you must wake up each and every day with the mindset to win. Get your offensive and defensive mind intact and play the game with all your heart! Play to win!

WAKE UP THE GOALS & PASSIONS – Stand up, wake up, and shake yourselves! Search your heart and mind. What job would you do for free? That's most likely your passion. As I stated early, I've spoken at many well-known places pro bono. These include the Department of Treasury, the Library of Congress, the U.S. Census Bureau, Quantico Marine Base and the list goes on. Why you may ask? Simply, because I *love* empowering others!

I love the joy that something I say may cause people to move from where they are to where they need to be. For I've always desired to do just that. What would you do for free if you were debt-free or not? Then this is what you should be pursuing daily. Work what you must for now from 9AM to 5PM and work what you love from 5PM to 9PM. Continue to do this until you can drop the day job and began to do what you love full time. (A lesson told to me by my savvy nephew Quinn)

CHALLENGE YOURSELF – You must challenge yourself each and every day.
Don't become complacent in any environment. *Shake the very foundations of the places you find yourself.* I challenge myself yearly at different conferences. I love presenting this topic, "Do it **Afraid**" but when the conference chairperson

informs me that they need seminars on the topic of leadership and communication, I accept the challenge. I prepare briefings on them both and present them. They are well received.

I also have begun presenting at Science, Technology, Engineering and Math (STEM) conferences as well. This was even more challenging, for they provide you with the topics, desired objectives and outcomes and you must develop a briefing accordingly. This was very challenging for me, but I love challenges, I guess from having competed in sports most of my life. So, don't be afraid to accept challenges that come your way, for they will grow and mature you in your perspective brand.

WORK ON YOUR WEAKNESSES – I've already stated earlier that simple acknowledgment for me is how I overcome my weakness. However, I'm also aware that even in loving to speak and motivate others, I have room to grow in this area. No matter how many times I do it, fear always seem to rise up at the time I'm about to stand up.

Also, I do know of some who have desires and a passion for particular things that they may not perform as well as they'd like. To you, I encourage you to work on those weaknesses. Take time to practice daily or weekly on those things until you become totally comfortable in performing them. But if you are like me, you will never become totally comfortable. I'm simply doing it afraid.

DO THINGS DIFFERENTLY – Don't do things the way you've *always* done them. If it works, great, but you can make changes and improvements on that which is working. It would be absurd to continue to use handouts only in my seminars instead of implementing power point slides as well. I know we've been taught, if it's not broke, don't fix it. But we all would benefit from embracing the changing technology. Not the same thing works for everyone. So, discover what works best for you and the audience you are attempting to reach and implement. We must be willing to make wise changes when necessary, for change is truly inevitable. Realize people learn differently as well. *A teacher doesn't know what s/he has taught until the students tell them what they've heard.*

SET NEW GOALS – I cannot stress enough the importance of setting new goals in both your personal and professional life. If you set none, you will become stale and no longer relevant to the audience you seek to reach. Even in your personal goals, you must set some and then plan strategic ways in how you will achieve them. Have a roadmap in place. Give yourself deadlines and timelines. In order to stay relevant you must be willing to set new, attainable goals.

MOTIVATE YOURSELF – In the past, you may have depended upon others to validate and motivate you to help you keep performing or move to the next level. But at some point in life, which is now, you must learn to motivate yourself! Realize that others are struggling with their own situations and sometimes they aren't in the mood to motivate.

They are simply trying to stay afloat and swim until you or others come and rescue them. Realize there is fire on the inside of you. There is greatness inside and all over you. What you need, you already possess internally. Tap into it! Also know that many times, those who once motivated you have now become jealousy of you, because they never anticipated that you would rise to the level you have today. Your season with them is over.

Don't continue to pursue and stay in a dissolved relationship. This will stunt your growth, hinder your success, and clip your wings to fly. You must recognize this early. Therefore, it is paramount that you motivate yourself from this point forward. King David, so says the Bible, encouraged himself in the Lord. He even danced and praised the Lord so until he came out of his clothes. You are in David's bloodline. Therefore, an encourager is on the inside of you as well. Embrace him and allow him to break free in you!!!

CHAPTER SEVEN

CAUSES OF DEPRESSION

UNFULFILLING CAREERS – Many people are working in fields and careers that bring them little to no joy at all. Once upon a time, I too, was one of those people. If you are not a morning person already, then having to get up and prepare for a job that you strongly dislike is even more stressful.

Often, when I ask for a show of hands of those who are unfulfilled in their careers, every hand goes up. I'm always in awe. For I thought I was alone in my feeling unfulfilled. Not. The numbers are staggering of those who seek new careers. But due to longevity and other factors, they stay there as they become more depressed day-by-day. Don't allow yourself to get caught or stuck in a career that is unfulfilling. Be willing to move and try something new and different altogether.

DISAPPOINTMENTS ON THE JOB – Many people are suffering from a lot of disappointments on the job. It stems from lack of promotions, not taking enough vacations, long work hours, low pay, little to no benefits and high insurances. I've seen many quit good government jobs due to these particular factors.

We must learn to never function under stress. We should confront whatever is causing us stress and eliminate all of it or as much of it as possible. I tell people, take your vacations; the job will function without you. Trust me; just die. I've seen people die, we collect money to send a flower to their funeral and they are replaced the next day. Really. So, I say to you, take time off, take a lunch break, get up from your desk and walk outside to take a breather. *Balance is key.*

UNHEALTHY RELATIONSHIPS, BOTH IN OUR PERSONAL AND PROFESSIONAL LIFE – Too many of us hang out and converse with negative people and we fail to realize, they are the culprits of a lot of our stress, low self-esteem, and lack of drive for greater. I refuse to allow anyone, even in my family, to bring me down, talk me down, or belittle the greatness that is welling up on the inside of me! My struggle has been too long, too great, and too hard for me to revert back to seeking approval from those who never had my back in the first place. Let me say it differently, just fall on hard times, and see how many will come seeking to "comfort" and console you. But then just decide one day you are about to get up! Those many will turn to few then none.

There's something strange, very strange, about mankind that causes them to look down, belittle, become jealousy and envious of others when they see them rising. I don't understand for the life of me, why so much jealousy, especially in the body of Christ.

I've discovered that most people don't mind you getting and having, as long as you don't get and obtain more than they have. How foolish! I truly rejoice with everybody when I see them excel in their personal and professional lives and I weep with them when they weep. If you want to free yourself of stress and depression, start by checking your immediate circle. Either people are for you or against you. You should know how to distinguish between the two by now. A renowned pastor once told me, "Val, you will only have about one to two *genuine* friends in your entire life. Three if you are lucky. Because most people are typically jealousy and envious of each other's success." Well...as you see, I could stay here a while, but let's move on.

SHORTSIGHTED GOALS – Too often people set big goals and have dreams and they soon allow them to vanish. I called them shortsighted, because they never allow these goals to marinate in their minds as they plan a path forward to accomplish their goal. The goal may very well be their breakthrough, a great discovery, a witty invention, or some cure to a world's pain. But life, stress, and people began to play on the person's mind and allow him to forsake as well as abandon their goals. In order to stay relevant, you must set and pursue goals that are reachable and attainable.

LACK OF VISION & PATH FORWARD –
This is very similar and related to goals. I already stated that without a vision, the people perish so says the Bible. It's very important to have a vision of where you want to be in next two years, five years and what age you'd like to retire. If you don't plan for a retirement, you surely won't be able to retire comfortably. Resources and all other matters must be well thought out and planned.

In your relationships, if you have been dating someone for years and they are not ready to marry and commit to you, I'd say, keep'a stepping. Don't belittle who you are or sacrifice your desires based on others who are connected to you, but are not ready to move forward. Again, you may have to drop some dead weight to effectively move forward. As actor and film producer Tyler Perry said, "Learn the gift of goodbye."

UNFULFILLED IN PERSONAL LIFE –
Many people are unfulfilled in their personal lives and ultimately it manifests in their professional lives. I'm a firm believer that I will never be the best in my professional careers as an engineer, motivational speaker, preacher, writer, and non-profit director until I get free and healed of all of my personal struggles and setbacks.

Too often, I believe we see an outburst in school shootings, violence upon children political breakdowns, and other arenas all because people have failed to get their personal lives in check. Trying to hide and cover those things in our lives or past that bring embarrassment to us is perhaps not the most effective way to deal with them. We must develop and cultivate healthy relationships in our personal lives so that we can flourish and excel in our professional lives.

CHAPTER EIGHT

DEPRESSION TURNED OUTWARD

LESS PROACTIVE ON THE JOB – Whenever we are battling any form of depression, it is guaranteed to manifest in our professional lives. One of the key and most revealing signs is that we become less driven in our careers.

I must confess, there were times when depression had me so weighted down that I wasn't as productive on the job as I should have been. I believe many suffer with depression daily and signs of outbursts are screaming to us all that these people need help. Many people commit suicide as their last resort to find peace. However, we must be cognizance of those who we work with, and make it known when we know they are not acting as their usual selves.

NO EXCITEMENT IN CAREER – Many have loss the excitement that they once had for their career. If you ask them about their job, their reply is short and you might receive and answer that it's okay, it's a job, or that it pays the bills. They feel useless and you will find that they call in sick a lot or may just go absent without leave (AWOL).

Far too many people are sacrificing their health, their family's well being and even their company's growth by not just sitting down with their supervisor and confessing they don't like their current job. I realize not every office has the flexibility to move people from one branch to another if they stated such a fact, but there should be some alternative solution to your employer allowing you to work in a job that you enjoy and brings fulfillment.

DREAD GETTING UP – Wow! I can't tell you the countless time I have asked how many people dread getting up in the morning to go to their current jobs and *every* hand goes up. And some people raise both hands! People are living with so much dread in their lives due to their depression, failures, and unfulfilled lives. It may not always show either as people have learned to wear facades to cover their true feelings and emotions. I'm at a loss of words when I see the hands, because I too, lived and worked with a spirit of dread daily. It's overwhelming and very depressing within itself.

However, you must know that you can no longer stay in dread. Dread is like procrastination, it robs you of your full potential to live a fulfilling life. Let go of all dread and simply pursue a new course that brings joy back into your life.

BECOMING COMFORTABLE WHERE WE ARE – Too often we find our comfort zone and live, work, play and die right there.

Yet I tell people to never allow your self to become comfortable in an uncomfortable situation. Once I had to make a commute from Virginia to Maryland, rising at 3AM, leaving my house by 4AM, driving to a commuter lot to board a van with strangers I might add, just to get to work by 7AM.

I thought to invest in a neck pillow as many of the van riders had to make this uncomfortable situation more comfortable meanwhile. But I heard this, "If you are expecting me to change your job situation and give you a job closer to home, why then are you planning to buy a neck pillow? *Don't attempt to make yourself comfortable in an uncomfortable situation.*" Needless to say, I never invested in one of those pillows and my situation soon changed. I landed a new job much closer to home! Seek change.

LOSE DRIVE FOR SUCCESS – Most people are not driven in their personal or professional lives. People desire change, but are not always willing to do what's necessary for change to take place. I must testify, even if you are currently in a job that brings no fulfillment, don't stop performing at your level best.

For example, I was used to receiving all A's during appraisal time and once after about 16 years of employment, my supervisor changed, and the new supervisor graded me as a B. I went to him and talked to him trying to understand why he thought my work was a B level and not an A.

After much talking, it still didn't make sense to me and I left his office mad. By the time I made it back to my desk I told myself this, "If he thinks I'm performing at a B level then I'm getting ready to do less work and try to work on a B level." For I was sure I had performed at an A level. But I heard this in my spirit, "*You must keep performing at a high level, not for where you are but for where you are going.*" Wow!

What a revelation! Yes, I kept performing at a high level and I was soon flying right up out of there and landed a great job elsewhere, many miles away in a new state!

Once I landed my new job, I began to receive National Awards, big bonuses, and recognition far greater than I had ever received before. Mind you, I had spent less time on this job. However, I was sure that because I chose to keep a positive mindset at the previous place and kept performing, it now was paying off at my new job. So, I say to you, you cannot lose your drive for success. Keep performing until someone else notices your work. And if perhaps they don't, this may truly be a sign that you need to start your own business.

Too many people who have great leadership skills are making others rich. Be brave! Take the skills you've utilized for all those years making other companies great and start your own brand! We've been taught, go to school, get a degree, join the military, land a job, start a family, buy a house and live happily ever after. But no one has taught us to be entrepreneur-minded and start our own business. Go for it TODAY! Yes, you have what it takes!

CHAPTER NINE

HOW TO OVERCOME DEPRESSION

RECOGNIZE & ADMIT THE FEELINGS
— If you plan to get well, you must first recognize that you are depressed and be willing to admit it. I don't mean you must go telling everyone you see that you are depressed. No, but confiding in a close family member or friend would be ideal. Everyone doesn't have your best interest at hand. Some people will take what you've shared and use it against you, especially if it means beating you out of a promotion over them.

The key and most important factor is to realize that you are different, that you don't feel the same, and tell someone. They may not be able to help you, but they most likely will be able to refer you to the right spiritual leader or counselor who can provide the help you need. Too many times we suffer in silence and many go lacking because of it. I believe many arguments, disagreements and relationships breakdown could be avoided if we all strived to be whole individuals.

DISCOVER THE CAUSES – Not only is it good to recognize and admit that you are depressed, but it's key into finding out why you are depressed. All of us suffer depression, sometimes weekly as the chemical balance in our bodies change, a pet dies, we lose love ones, relationship break down, etc. The key is not whether we will ever experience depression, but to not stay there. It's all right to cry and shed many tears, but one must not make this a way of life. Be honest with yourself and confess the true reasons of why you are depressed. No doubt you will then get the precise care and attention that you need.

SEEK HELP – After admitting that you are depressed and all the reasons why, it's so instrumental that you seek professional help. This help may come in the form of your local pastor, grief ministry at church or a psychologist. I know professional help can be very expensive and many times this is why we never pursue it. But realize that your wellbeing is vital to you keeping your job and sometimes your relationships. Be willing to reach out to some form of counselor to share your story. It's not always easy at first to pour out your heart to those whom you don't know, but you will be the better for it in the end. Always seek help when feeling depressed for any length of time.

BE WILLING TO TALK ABOUT IT – The very last thing you want to do is internalize your feelings when you are depressed. You must seek out people who have your best heart, health and interest at hand and pour out your heart to them. This may only be one or two people, but you must talk about what's going on inside.

Too many people are suffering from stress-induced illnesses all because they fail to talk about what's going wrong on the inside of them. People are not mind readers. No one will automatically know you are hurting if you don't verbalize it. Sure, people can tell you are not yourself, but it makes getting you help so much easier and quicker if you are willing to state what's going on in your life. Share wisely, but please share.

MOVE FORWARD – Once you have sought help, you must be willing to move forward. Depression is never easy, but the key is to get back up again and keep moving. Day-by-day, you will find yourself returning to yourself. Involve yourself in fun activities that you once did, maybe bowling, swimming, working out, long walks, reading and anything that makes you feel good about you.

As much as possible, seek to get outside and enjoy the sunshine, snow or fall leaves. Nature has a way of soothing us and making us feel good. Even if you only take one small step daily, take that step with confidence and the next day will be even a bigger step. Disassociate yourself with negative people and environments that bring you down. You are in a healing process, so your surroundings are key. Keep moving forward!

SEEK REWARDING CAREERS – It's very important that you do not continue to settle for a job that brings you absolutely no joy. Realize that life is short and death is sure! By the time you learn how to live, it will then be time to die. Don't settle in any area of your life. There is something that you do well and very well. But you must be willing to chase it down and pursue it with everything in you. *Don't allow other people's fears to become your fears.*

Some people desire to go higher, but their fear of failure or perhaps their fear of success grips them and keep them bound. But you, yes, the one who chose to read this book, obviously know that destiny is calling you to come higher. You cannot remain in the same place and live with a spirit of dread. So, I challenge you today to arise, to pursue your goals, passions and dreams. And if you fail the first few times, get back up, dust yourself off, and strategize and go after it again.

FOCUS ON ACCOMPLISHMENTS – You have accomplished so much in life and don't think on these things as some small thing. Your strengths are evident and you have mastered them quite well. Don't ever forget about the great and mighty things you have accomplished both in your personal and professional life. You were born to win and soar at high heights. In doing so, don't allow others to down play or minimize the accolades you have achieved.

They speak for themselves, but you must keep them at the forefront of your mind for those low days.

CHAPTER TEN

HOW TO OVERCOME SHAME

REALIZE THAT TEMPORARY DEFEATS ARE ONLY TEMPORARY

We all have experienced fear, failure, depression and emotions that bring about shame. Notice that I didn't discuss the causes of shame, because the list is unending of the many things and ways shame engulfs us and our psyche; from very simple things to major things. Shame is inevitable. So, once again, it's not whether we will ever be made to feel shame but how we process and deal with it.

I can remember once that I was in the beauty shop waiting for my stylist to wash my hair. To my surprise, due to her busyness, she prompted for this young lady to shampoo my hair. Well...I wasn't used to this. I wasn't used to one person washing and another person styling my hair, so my face must have shown some disgust with the idea. I was not prepared for what would happen next. The young lady noticed my facial expression obviously and from across the entire salon, she begin to shout, "Hey, you don't want me to wash your hair, then I don't have to wash your hair because I'm still going to get paid whether I wash your hair or not!" Not to mention she was rolling her head and neck as she talked. Wow, you're talking about SHAME!

Everybody in the shop turned to look at to whom was she speaking. And I sat there, looking cheap by now, feeling embarrassed, trying not to appear upset so I simply ignored her, realizing she was much younger than I. But she continued. Yes, I was ashamed and that was definitely my last visit at that shop. I now have people dying laughing when I share this story, because you'd have to know how she was talking and pronouncing the words to get the full effect of what happened that day. Yet, I realize that was only temporary. I did not and chose not to go back there to get my hair done so I won. You must know temporary defeats are truly only temporary.

Don't label your entire life as a defeated one if you've experienced both wins and losses. It's part of the game called life. I've lost at many of things in life, but I never summed up my entire life as a defeated and failed one. Time has taught me that both sun and rain makes the grass and flowers grow. Without them both, the earth would not be in balance and yield its fruit and crop. We must stay in tune to which season we are currently in. It may be winter, spring, summer or fall in our lives. When you understand your *season of life,* then you can be better equipped with what's needed for the journey.

RECOGNIZE THE UNIQUE VALUE ONE HAS TO OFFER

You should know by now that you have something very unique and special to offer in every setting you find yourself. Your gifts, talents, know-how, skills, and experience are needed every place you go. I've been blessed to have worked for the Army, Air Force and Navy. I took what I learned those sixteen years with the Army and applied those skill-sets with the Air Force. After leaving the Air Force, I embarked upon the Navy. I carried with me my tool bag that had both Army and Air Force knowledge in it. Even though my job assignments were different at all locations, some general and common professional, leadership and communication skills were consistent and needed for each branch of service.

No matter how small others have tried to make you feel or how small you may have felt yourself, it was not accurate. You and everyone around you have something very unique and special to offer. Everyone on the team is important. When we won a game, we won as a team; when we lost a game, we lost as a team.

Yes, I know we often contribute the win or loss to whomever made the last great play or bad play. But the entire game consisted of four quarters of play, not seconds only. So, it would be wise for us to not point fingers and do the blame game knowing we all played a part in the loss or win.

Don't ever allow others make you feel insecure or insignificant. You matter.

GET UP AGAIN!

You must not quit! Shame will come and embarrass us all from time-to-time. However, you must know that you are not considered a defeated foe as long as you get back up again. Life will sometimes knock you way down low, even to the ground, but it's temporary and all in how you view it. There have been times in my life that I was so low, I could have swung my feet off a sheet of paper. But I didn't stay there. I got back up again, over and over until I gained my balance. Once I was balanced, I began to crawl, then walk, later run and I now FLY!

You too have the power and the ability to fly right up out of those depressing and shameful situations and moments that you find yourself in. Once in 1999, my daughter and I were traveling home and we saw this dog as it lay on the side of the road; a car had hit it no doubt. As we approached it, it kept trying to get up, but it was obvious that all four of his legs were broken so he would just fall back to the ground. It was painful to look upon. I had to turn my head as we passed by.

Yet, my young daughter at that time, only four years old, said something soooooooo profound! She said, "M*ama, just like that dog, people all over the world are down and trying to get up.*" Can I tell you the Holy Spirit fell in our car and I began to weep like a baby? Out of the mouth of babes...!!! I truly know that flesh and blood did not reveal that to her!

People near and far, both nationally and internationally, and shades of many colors are down and trying to get up.

So I say to you, "Rise!!!"

People need what's inside of you! I need what's inside of you.

CHAPTER ELEVEN

CAUSES OF SETBACKS IN CAREERS & LIFE

BURN OUT – Many people are totally and completely tired and in fact sick and tired of their current jobs, their relationships, and even their surroundings. They have allowed themselves to stay in that low state for too long. Becoming burned out with life, people, and places to name of few of their distresses. They long to break free and experience fulfillment in all areas of their lives, but the stress of life have beaten them down.

Some people even quit their jobs right in the middle of their careers with no plan for where they will go next. Some people are overwhelmed by their current tasks. Others are in what they consider a dead relationship and they are simply looking for a way out. Burnouts must be recognized and dealt with immediately or else they can cause major blowouts and breakdowns in other areas of our lives.

POOR PERFORMANCE ON THE JOB – Too often, people show up at work, but do nothing once there. Others do very little on the job due to overwhelming circumstances in their personal or professional lives.

They desire to perform, but due to their depression, failures, and shame, they simply go through the motion.

Many people, after receiving poor ratings, fall into even greater depths of depressions. Every setback in a person's life will manifest in their professional life. It's vital to seek help when you know you have loss your drive to perform and excel on your job. Live life to the fullest; don't just drift through it.

LACK OF PROMOTIONS – I know of people who have worked twenty and thirty plus years in their perspective fields and have never received a raised on their jobs. I wonder how is this even possible. Especially when health insurances, food, gas and other basic needs have only increased year after year. Yet, they have remained faithful to those jobs, showing up daily and on time, working because they have a family to care for back home. Some have died on the job, having heart attacks and strokes as I'm sure were due to stress and being over worked.

Most of their wages went towards high insurance premiums that covered very little in the form of healthcare, so they still found themselves out of money during doctor visits. We must never allow others to take advantage of our skill-sets and produce wealth for themselves and their companies, while we remain house poor. We must be willing to pursue jobs and careers that offer great benefits, great hours and time off from the job. Better yet, we must learn to be entrepreneurs!

FEELING OVERWHELMED WITH TASKS - A lot of people have many gifts and talents and don't know how to say no. They take on responsibilities and tasks that cause them to become overwhelm. However, instead of telling spouses, children, spiritual leaders and supervisors that they are way in over their head, they press forward trying to achieve all that's been assigned to them. Parents sign their children up for every sporting event and play at school. Not realizing that when one seasonal sport ends, another begins which means they will constantly have to run their children from here to there and attend their events after work.

Spiritual leaders have tasked us to serve as overseer on boards or committees and we feel that we must say yes. Supervisors have deadlines and schedules that they must meet and they depend upon us to provide the program reviews. We must find some quality time to spend with our spouses, children and significant other. We must learn to balance our lives and schedules.

LACK OF COMMUNICATION – It is said that most marriages end due to lack of communication. Communication is so critical when dealing with others in your personal and professional lives. In my seminar entitled "Effective" Communication and Leadership, I bring home the fact that all communication is not positive nor effective. Adolph Hitler was a leader and a communicator, but what he communicated had a very negative impact for the Jews. We must understand that 90% of communication is body language while 10% is what people say. That's strange, because people do so much talking these days, but if you desire to know what they are really saying, watch their body language. We must be great communicators on the job, in our homes and whatever setting we find ourselves.

When we assume that others know what we are thinking or feeling, we make a grave mistake. In order to keep relationships flowing smoothly, we must effectively communicate what we are saying, thinking or feeling. Some people communicate best verbally, others, written and still others by actions. We must communicate these known facts; for if we fail to realize this, then one would think the other is failing to communicate simply because s/he is not communicating the exact same way the other is communicating. We must truly say what we mean and mean what we say. Keep the lines open.

PERSONAL SETBACKS – Life, tragedies, deaths, and the many unknowns have touched all of our lives. We all have experienced personal tragedies that have caused us to mourn and grieve, sometimes beyond words. I often say that I wish life was such that when my Mom passed, that my job would have allowed me three to six months paid time off to heal from her death. But no, life isn't that way. Yes, if I had that type of leave, I could use it, but if not, then I would have to either report back to work sooner than desired or take leave without pay. I don't know too many people nowadays who can afford the latter.

So, we show up at work, church, the gyms, market places, etc. with all of our grief, burdens, and brokenness. No one can see our heart and know the pain that we are experiencing. Too many suffer in silence until they have some extreme outburst in the forms of road rage, yelling and screaming at the kids or spouse, and being irritable at work. Many times the one grieving has suffered too long and need the attention of a professional counselor. We must seek help in the onset when we are experiencing low times in life; for many smile through their pain.

LACK OF VACATIONS - I've already stated that people don't take enough vacations. Many government employees have "use or lose leave" at the end of each year, and some people lose their leave instead of donating it or simply using it. I don't understand this. I refuse to lose leave when I have shown up at work daily and on time, performed my tasks, traveled for the job and made a difference. I will continue to say, the job will go on without you and I.

Some think they are irreplaceable and that their projects will not get completed without them. Just die. I've also heard of people having heart attacks and strokes right in their seats at work.

People, take your vacations. Learn to get away from the job; from being a stay-at-home Mom and take a long, needed vacation. You will be the better for it both now and later.

CHAPTER TWELVE

WHAT TO DO IN A SETBACK

FACE IT & START OVER – All of us have experienced disappointments in some area of our lives. The key is not to focus on the thing or people that caused your disappointments. You must deal with the setback and be willing to start over again. Sometimes we experience setbacks in our lives due to our own mistakes.

What happens to us at work, home and in life is not always other people's fault. It takes maturity and growth to acknowledge that you were at fault. Yet, be the bigger man or woman, boy or girl and acknowledge to others when you are at fault. It will reveal your strength, not your weakness. Starting over in anything can be worrisome and bring about dread. However, if you want something bad enough, you must be willing to work at it until you get it right.

There were times I had started a book or a paper only to find out my computer crashed and I didn't save the work as I had thought. Starting from scratch was not something I desired nor looked forward to doing. Yet, I had to do just that. Instead of pouting, complaining, blaming others, I sucked it up and began to type again from scratch. Be willing to start over. Even publishing this book has caused me much grief. Yet I can't quit until it's complete.

SEEK NEW PATHS TO SUCCEED – After you face your setback and start over, the next key is to seek new paths to succeed. Even if you are attempting the same thing that you once failed in, do research and study your craft. Gain all the knowledge possible in going forward in your pursuit.

Sometimes failures denote that we are pursuing the wrong thing. Other times, if we know that what we are pursuing is our passion then in this case, press forward. Always look for new ideas, new strategies and approaches when moving forward.

MAJOR ON YOUR STRENGTHS – Always focus on those areas that you do well with little to no effort whatsoever. We all have strengths and weaknesses, but maximize your strengths. As an example, I feel that I have developed my motivational speaking skill-set tremendously by accepting many engagements that offered no honorarium. To be paid for my gift each time I accepted an engagement would have been awesome.

However, I've always seen those opportunities as chances for me to hone in on my speaking skills and make all the rough edges smooth. I always grow and learn during and after every speaking engagement. Every crowd is different. Their needs are different.

But what has remained consistent for me is I thrive to have a greater impact each and everyone every time I stand to speak. My approach is that I always go in expecting to leave with more engagements than when I walked in. And almost always, that is the case. You must demonstrate your excitement and joy in sharing whatever your brand is. You must believe in yourself and what you have to offer 100%!!! Your willingness to serve in your brand for free until people can pay is a definite sign this is your passion. So work your strengths.

MINOR IN THE INSIGNIFICANT ISSUES - So what if you failed in this area or another. We all have failed. Many people's failures are public while other people's failures are private. It doesn't matter; the same outcome is true for us all. We tend to feel shame, become depressed and experience other negative emotions. The key is to recognize and deal with those feelings immediately. Don't focus on your failures or your weaknesses.

The mere fact that you got back up again is proof you are not a failure. The easiest thing in life to do is quit, give up and go soak in your pity party. But the wise thing to do is admit your weaknesses, accept defeat for that moment and get back up with purpose and determination. Life will throw many curve balls at you daily.

You must learn how to use your strengths to hit them and use wisdom as you move from base to base. Remember, *you don't have to be able to run fast if you can hit a home run.*

ACCEPT ONE'S RESPONSIBILITY FOR THE SETBACK - One of the biggest problem with so many and why they never move forward is because they blame someone or everyone else for their own mistakes. As we grow physically, we should also be growing spiritually and emotionally. We should always be willing to take an honest inventory of our current situations and see where we may have caused the breakdown.

On every basketball team I played, I would hit girls upside the head with the ball, because they weren't expecting me to throw it since I wasn't telegraphing my pass. I observed Magic Johnson with the no-look pass and developed my skills to do the same pass. I did. But many times, I ended up with five or more turnovers on my stats all because the girls never caught my pass. Not only that, I would always say, "my bad" as we ran back to play defense when I really knew it was their fault because they were wide open. I'm in no ways implying you should accept the blame for things when it's obvious that it's another fault. What I am saying is, always be big and mature enough to admit when it is your fault.

DEAL WITH IT – Now that you've admitted your faults, deal with it. Ways to deal with your setbacks are: try different and new approaches, do research on your brand and network with others who are doing what you desire to do. Be willing to shadow others who are doing what you love to do. Get training, attend workshops and be open regarding the areas in which you lack strong knowledge. Never, ever isolate yourself. Stay connected to positive people and go-getters in life!!!

CHAPTER THIRTEEN

HOW TO TURN EVERY *SET*BACK INTO A *COME*BACK

ACKNOWLEDGE ONE'S FAULTS

We all have the power to speak things into existence in our lives. We can choose to speak negative things or positive things, but daily we speak one or the other. We all have failed in life in many things. Some have failed many times in multiple areas. We all have made mistakes in our relationships with girlfriends, boyfriends, spouses, family members, coworkers and the list goes on.

One of the easiest things to do when relationships fail is to blame someone else for the breakdown. But if we truly plan to heal and go forward, we must stop and tell others when we are at fault for the breakdown. We must acknowledge that we over re-acted, spoke wrongly or unkindly, or simply misunderstood all that was going on. It takes a mature person to do this. Not one who is weak, but one who is meek. One who realizes that there's good and bad in us all.

I cannot tell you how many times I've gone to others and apologized for things I said and did or did not say and did not do to cause my part of the breakdown in the failed relationships. Now, whether they accepted my many apologies weren't always clear, but one thing for sure, I felt lighter, better and complete liberty. I knew then I could live with a clear conscious for whatever I did. Now that I've apologized, I can move on.

When we fail to recognize and admit our faults, we become harden and a very bitter person in life. When we walk around with the attitude that everyone else is wrong and have done us wrong, our view is cloudy and distorted. We think the worse about all people that we come into contact with. We don't trust anyone, even those who are worthy of being trusted; all because our own behavior have caused the breakdown.

If you plan to turn every setback in your life into a comeback, you must acknowledge your errors when you see them or when they are brought to your attention. Even on your job, acknowledge to others when you have taken the low road and misspoke or blew something out of proportion. People will respect you for your genuineness and relationships will have the opportunity to mend a lot faster. Be the bigger person, go and make right the things you realize you are responsible for.

MASTER ONE'S WEAKNESSES

I will say once more that for myself, acknowledging my weaknesses are one of the best ways I master them. However, I also like to work on my weaknesses when time permits me the opportunity to do so. I recall being a great ball handler and won many ball handling ribbons at Ole Miss basketball camps. I had mastered the Magic Johnson no-look pass, as long as I passed with both hands or with my right hand. But when it came to dribbling with my left hand, I would always lose the ball out of bounds. Any great defensive player knows to get on the point guard's strong side and make her have to dribble to her weak side. Each time while going left, I either loss the ball out of bounds or it was stolen from me.

But my coach started working with me in the gym daily in my early high school years, putting blinders on me and tying my right hand behind my back forcing me to dribble with my left hand. This was very, very uncomfortable at first. But each day, I got stronger with my left hand until one day I noticed I could control the ball with my left hand without looking down while I dribbled. I eventually learned to pass with my left hand running full speed down court. I would just lift the ball up and also pass it. I mastered dribbling and even passing behind my back; smooth bounce passes with my left hand. And perhaps those great ball-handling skills were what eventually afforded me the opportunity to take my skills professionally overseas.

What am I saying, work on your weaknesses until you master them. If your weakness is an area you never plan to use or pursue, then maybe you can get by without working on it. But skill-sets that you know you will need in life; I'd say work on them as much as time permits. However, keep in mind, this skill may never become a strength and that's okay. The key is to recognize your weaknesses and be willing to acknowledge them. Surround yourself with people who possess strengths that are your weaknesses.

DON'T BE AFRAID TO COMEBACK

If you really plan to turn every one of your setbacks into a comeback, you *cannot* be afraid to come back. You must know that people fail every day and people get back up again every day. Many people never get back up, because they figure it's easier to accept defeat and pretend they didn't really want whatever they were pursuing anyway. Simply, they were just testing the waters, trying something new and being adventurous.

Quitting is easy, but it's not acceptable. You must get up, dust yourself off and be more determined than ever before to pursue your goals. Whatever is worth having is worth working for. *Sometimes with much sweat and tears only will you see your dreams come to pass.* Be willing to look foolish to others. Be willing to start over from scratch if need be. Be willing to succeed at all cost. You must be willing to stand and stand alone even in very difficult times.

Seasons come and seasons go, you won't be in winter season forever. Know that your spring and summer season are closer than you think. Take your eyes and mind off the critics, the naysayers, and those who told you wouldn't succeed in the first place. They looked for you to fail, give up and quit. However, prove them wrong. Show them what you are made of. Let them see the real man or woman you are at the core. You were born to win! You were born to dream! You were born to fly at high heights. Take your place. Now arise.

CHAPTER FOURTEEN

SOARING HIGH IN YOUR CAREER & LIFE

MAXIMIZE YOUR TIME – If you plan to soar high in your career and in life, you must learn to maximize your time. Your time is very important and what you do with it daily is crucial. Ways to maximize your time are: seek out highly motivated people to surround yourself with; research your craft or brand and discover new ways to work them; be creative and innovative with your brand; use your strengths to your advantage; on every opportunity be open to learn from others and lastly network, network, network.

Time is something you will never get back. We all are given the same amount daily; however, many use their time wrong and complain that there just isn't enough time in a day to get done what's needed. Time is not the issue.

The problem is we need to prioritize the things we need to complete and get done in each day. Networking with others at conferences and other venues is key. You must be willing to use your time wisely on a daily basis.

Many times I have been flying and boarded the aircraft only to get delayed due to weather or mechanical issues. They never de-board us. They only make us sit there for hours on the runway until the problem is fixed. Instead of complaining, bickering, whine and be obnoxious, I use that time to write. I have learned to maximize my time daily realizing things may not always go as planned.

Be prepared for breakdowns, let downs, and disappointments to happen in your life daily. Part of being prepared is using that time to work on yourself and your brand. If everything goes smoothly and as planned for you each day, that's even better; but typically, that's not the case. So, learn to maximize your time daily.

PROMOTE YOURSELF – The main reason you need to network is to promote your gifts, talents and abilities to others. You may be the best in your craft or have the latest upcoming technology, speech, or brand. However, if you don't showcase your brand to others, people will never know how great you are. I've heard and seen that if you are great, you don't need to advertise. And people use Bentleys and Rolls Royce's cars as example. We never see a commercial where they are advertising their cars, yet they still sale many of them. Yet the average business, no matter what they are selling, will always advertise. So, don't underestimate the power of advertisement.

Have you ever noticed that whenever a restaurant advertises their food on television, you are more prone to stop by there to check out the latest dish you saw advertised? It's amazing, because advertisement is very, very powerful. I can remember that once, I attended a conference and my name didn't make the booklet about my upcoming workshop. So, I printed out flyers and stopped everyone in the convention center's hallway to advertise my upcoming seminar that would take place the next morning. Not only was it the next morning, but it was at 8AM.

I wanted people to attend, because I knew they would benefit from the things I had to share. I was way out of my comfort zone to be handing out flyers promoting myself this way, but guess what, it worked! It seemed that every one that I handed a flyer to the day before showed up bright and early for my 8AM seminar as it was packed. I was shocked and thrilled all at the same time. I asked them what made them come and many simply told me they had sat in a previous seminar of mine and others said they had heard of me before.

Who knows, maybe I didn't have to advertise like that after all, but I'm glad I did as it helped me to come out of my comfort zone.

So, whenever possible, promote yourself to others. I struggle in this area, because whereas I know what I have to offer, I don't want to come across as bragging or being arrogant to others.

However, if you are humble with your greatness, others will see it and desire to support you whenever possible.

DON'T BE AFRAID OF FAILURE – In order to truly soar high in your career and personal life, you must not be afraid of failure in any form. Many people who have overcome great odds didn't start out that way. Actress and singer Jennifer Hudson did not win when she appeared on American Idol.

Yet she didn't allow the people's opinion of her singing voice derail or stop her desires to keep moving forward. She went on to audition for the movie Dream Girls and not only did she beat out previous American Idol winners, but she landed one of the leading roles in the movie.

It is said that some of the greatest inventions and witty ideas are in the grave. There are many who died with goals, dreams, and inventions still lying dormant within them. They never launched out to attempt their dream, passions, and goals due to fear or perhaps lack of resources. Don't let the same be said about you. You have many great ideas inside of you that are waiting to be birthed. You must take the time and tap into them.

The world is waiting for what you have to offer. If you try something and don't succeed, get back up again. Learn from you error and failure. Just don't quit. Be willing to rise every time you fall.

Life is full of wins and losses. Sometimes we win and sometimes we lose.

> *Bobby Jones said "I never learned one thing whenever I won a tournament."*

This tells me it's our losses that we learn from, not our wins. No one wins every time just as no one loses all the time. Life gives us both. We must learn to carry a great attitude and outlook on life whether we win or lose. Fear is inevitable, but you can face it or run from it. I choose to face all of my fears before I leave this earth. I want to leave no stone unturned in this area. You must stop fearing failure if you desire to soar high.

DON'T BE AFRAID OF SUCCESS – I will confess up front that fear of success has always been a great fear of mine, right behind my fear of public speaking. And for those that know me, they know I'm now a Motivational Speaker and Ordained Minister so I do quite a bit of public speaking. I was determined to overcome this fear. I still have not. I simply face this fear each time I rise to speak.

Most reasons that people give for their fear of success are: they fear drawing wrong people, they fear not being able to maintain that level of success, they fear not being able to handle the money and they fear what will be required to stay at the top of the success ladder. I have feared so many things in life that it almost scares me now.

I never wanted to draw a lot of attention to myself. And we all know, if you are very successful, you will draw a lot, a whole lot of attention. However, if you are going to soar high in your life, you must let go of all of your fears of success. Fear has no place it our lives. It is was once said, *"Fear is a state of nervousness only fit for children. Men should not fear. The only thing a man should fear is God. To fear anything other than God offends God."*

BE YOUR OWN CHEERLEADER! - If you are going to soar high in your personal and professional life you *must* be your own and best cheerleader! When we were young, we sought the approval of parents, teachers, coaches, etc. in life. However, as we matured in life, we then began to seek the approval of a desired significant other or spouse. Society teaches us to seek the approval of others.

For those of us who have involved ourselves in sports, we're accustomed to cheerleaders on the sideline cheering our team on whether we were losing or winning. The cheerleaders pumped up the crowd to cheer us on as well. This type of cheering could go to one's head hearing your name screamed and yelled out by them.

However, as we mature and advance in our different roles, positions and professions in life, we can no longer await the approval or cheers of others to validate our moves in life. We must spend time evaluating what move we should make next and be willing to make it without the loud claps and cheers from others. We must know that without a shadow of doubt, we are advancing in the right direction.

Many grown people have become stuck in life, because they are awaiting the approval from others in their inner circle and some from their outer circle. Some people are not able to move forward because they seek the great approval of one person whom they look up to and admire greatly.

We all must learn and learn fast that many people are dealing with their own storms in life. They are consumed by the peaks and valleys that life take them through. People sometimes refuse to motivate and cheer you on, especially if you seem to be advancing beyond them. Many people operate in jealousy in the workplace, church, and other venues that we find ourselves. Jealousy will keep people from motivating you when they see you thriving in life. Therefore, learn to motivate yourself daily from this point forward.

CHAPTER FIFTEEN

DO "IT" AFRAID!

DON'T BE AFRAID TO OUTSHINE OTHERS

By now you should know what "it" is. It is whatever goal, passion or dream that you desire and fear is keeping you from attempting to achieve it. You cannot be afraid to outshine others in your circle or larger circles. Remember you have both strengths and weaknesses. Acknowledge your weaknesses and perform your strengths as though you are the only one who can do those things well.

You must always shine and shine bright. I tell the story that once I lit a candle with an already lit candle in my candle. I notice the candle I used to light the other candle began to shine brighter and brighter as it touched the other candle. A word for you: don't be afraid to shine bright and always be willing to light other's light. Your light will not go dim or out, it will only shine brighter. At the same time never allow others to minimize the light that you carry. Never allow another to minimize the value you have to offer.

Sometimes you will have to shine brighter than your family, friends and close acquaintances. If they truly love you for who you are, they will encourage you to maximize the greatness that's within you and you should be encouraging them just the same.

STOP SHRINKING TRYING TO FIT IN WITH OTHERS

Never shrink in any setting trying to make others feel big about themselves. There truly is nothing in the world enlightening about shrinking. It doesn't benefit you or the people around you. As we started in life, many of us shrunk trying hard not to outshine others. But at this late date in your life, you cannot afford to shrink in life.

Shrinking doesn't look good on you. You must rise and go forward in life. You have greatness living on the inside of you. You have grand ideas and something/s that you do very well. Instead of shrinking trying hard not to intimidate others, rise and challenge others to come up where you are. Someone in your circle has to set the bar.

I've always heard if you are the smartest one in your circle, you need to find a new circle to hang out in. I always desire to be around others who have great wisdom and knowledge about life. I don't tolerate negative minded and negative talking people to engulf my space, life or ears. They drain me. I desire to be around people who are very positive and know what they want in life.

I thrive on giving back in life to others who are less fortunate and may not have had the opportunities that most of us have had. I gravitate towards people who are looking to advance and push others to another level.

While we should motivate ourselves, sometimes we need help in getting back up again from a fall in life. Many people have had their share of experiencing hard times. In order that they never give up hope or give in, we must give them the push they need. Sometimes it's a word, it may be a ride from here to there, it may be money or just a listening ear. Whatever their need is, be available and approachable. We all need to stay approachable in life on a daily basis.

PUT YOUR BEST "WING" FORWARD AND SOAR HIGH

I have often shared this story and people love it each and every time. When I ordered my brand new BMW 325ci series convertible as I built it online in 2006, I knew life was being grand to me. For I have always wanted a convertible since Jr. High school. I had traveled with my job to Las Vegas and once I returned, my car was sitting in the showroom floor shipped straight from Germany. I was thrilled.

My daughter and I drove away with this beautiful car and thanking God for his great blessings. As we drove down University Avenue with the top dropped, life truly felt that it had opened up for us and we were enjoying it immensely. Then all of a sudden, out of nowhere, a sparrow flew in front of my car and hit my bumper making a really loud thump. I was speechless. I quickly pulled over and jumped from the car along with my daughter.

I dare this bird to hit my brand new car before even making it home with it! I told my daughter to take a good look at my bumper to see if she saw a dent, but she was focused on the sparrow that lay on the ground apparently dead. I quickly redirected her thoughts and told her to not worry about the bird on the ground (even though I love birds), but focus on my car to help me discover any dents.

As we got back in the car, thankful that there were no dents on my car, I heard these next words. "Val, even though I didn't give that bird wings the length of an eagle (as pilots have seen eagles flying at 15,000+ feet), I did give it wings so that it could have flown higher than the height of your car. Yet it chose to fly at a low level and that's why it got hit.

You and my people get hit in life a lot of times, because people are mean and low down, but too many times, *you get hit in life simply because you are flying too low*." So, I challenge every reader today, rise and fly high!

Fly above your fears, rejection, depression, low self-esteem, shame and every setback! Rise and fly high and I'll meet you in the skies!!!

CONCLUSION

Every one that has ever lived in the world have experienced some type of fear, regardless of their race, age, cultural differences, or up-bringing. Some people fear flying, some dying, some heights, some public speaking, some starting a business, some starting a relationship, others ending a relationship and the list is unending. So, it doesn't matter the fear, the key is not to live in fear.

The first time I spoke at the Department of Treasury in Washington, D.C. I experienced great fear. As I had volunteered to speak for their 19th Financial Management annual program, I sat pondering moments before I had to speak, why did I set myself up like this.

As the Ronald Reagan ballroom began to fill with over 500 guests, fear began to overwhelm me like never before. I began to shake and it obviously showed. For the lady who had contacted me about coming to speak, leaned over and patted me on the hands as she told me I was going to do fine. I nodded attempting to agree with her, but inwardly, fear was getting the best of me.

I had prayed and fasted, but at that precise moment, neither seemed to have kicked in. Fear had consumed me, until I rose and faced the massive crowd and asked one key question. My question was simply this, "How many of you have fears in your life?" And to my amazement, every hand went high and many people near and far from where I stood raised both hands. It was at that particular moment all of my fears left me. I simply told them good, because I came to speak on fear and not finances. They all laughed which made me relax even more.

Afterwards, many people of all races came up to me, some crying, thanking me for being so transparent and telling me how my speech had spoken to them. It must have went pretty well for I was invited back to this same conference the next two years to speak in the same place on a different topic.

I was only able to obliged one of those engagements due to my schedule. I share this story to simple let you know, I've always feared public speaking, but in my adult years, I've long to overcome my fears. I don't think I will ever *overcome* my fears of public speaking; I'm simply *facing* them. If you plan to excel in life and allow life to get the very best out of you, you must face all of your fears also.

However, there is a *set* environment that you are *created* to perform in. The story is told about a man who purchased fish to restock his pond. Momentarily, he emptied the fish on the ground before putting them in the pond. He noticed how they flipped and flapped trying to breathe as long as they laid on the ground and he found this comical. But he noticed as soon as he put them in the water, the environment in which they were created to perform, they swam very majestically and with little to no effort at all.

If you are in an environment that causes you to "breathe" profusely and it seems the people are zapping the very life out of you, this may be a sign that you are in the wrong environment. Just like those fish, you too have a *created* environment that you were born to perform in with little to no effort of your own. The key is to find that environment however you must, land there and perform graciously. *Don't continue fighting to stay alive in an environment that's not conducive to whom you are and were created to be.*

I am a firm believer that "your gifts will make room for you and bring you before great men." (Proverbs 18:16) When you open up and allow your best to flow through and out of you, others will be drawn to you, your energy, and your positive flow. You won't have to fight to be seen or heard. People will seek you out and want your gift shared in their venues.

I'm amazed that most of my speaking engagements have come by way of referrals. I was referred to prestigious places like the Department of Treasury, the Library of Congress, U.S. Census Bureau and Quantico Marine Base. All of these places I've had the opportunity to speak twice. I never imagined I'd have such opportunities. What am I saying? If you will just step out of fear and do what comes natural to you, you will be sought after as well.

One point I really desire to bring home is that you must believe in yourself 100% and 100% of the time as you step out to "Do it **Afraid**!" For I recall being in high school and my shot was not the prettiest as I shot with both hands. I recall my coach telling me that he hopes the ball never ends up in my hand at the end of the game in a win or die situation. Due to his lack of faith in me, I lacked faith in myself even the more.

Well...guess what. Yes, it happened. It was the year 1982, I was a 10th grader and the starting point guard. We ended up in Jackson, MS to play in the state tournaments. I was fouled with less than ten seconds on the clock and we were down by two. As soon as I was fouled, I could hear my coach's word from practice really loud in my head. I felt his dread, along with my own as I walked to that free throw line. I wondered why did that girl have to foul me. I'd rather anybody else shoot the free throw, just not me. I refused to turn and look at the coach, knowing his face was probably in his hands.

I simply walked to that free throw line and with everything in me, I began to pep talk myself. I told myself to bend my legs low when I get ready to shoot as another girl does on the team. So, I did just that and I hit not one free throw, but both of them! Needless to say, the coach loved me that day, for a moment anyway. When I reflect back on the negative words I was told all season versus those two free throws at the end of the season, I realized that total confidence in oneself is needed in life to succeed and excel.

As long as I believed what others believed about me, I realize I would not succeed. But as soon as I decided to believe in myself, I was able to accomplish perhaps what I could have accomplished all season long. Yet too many times we allow other people's fears to become our fears. No more. I will not allow anyone to cast doubt in me, simply because they doubt themselves or me. Don't you do it either!

Life-Lesson Learned From Living

Some people would rather lose than admit they are wrong. Point and case: Once while I was in college playing basketball, we traveled to Tennessee to play a team. After showering and getting dressed, I was walking out of the locker room. However, I soon stopped in my tracks as I was shocked by what I was hearing. I heard our head coach cursing the media. We lost that game and she was upset that the media was interviewing our assistant coach verses her.

Well…I couldn't rest well at all on the long trip home. Something deep inside of me was telling me I had to confront her about her language to the media. After all, daily in practice she'd tell us that we're representing the Lady Chargers no matter where we go, even on weekends, therefore, to carry and handle ourselves accordingly.

Well, I felt the reverse was true also. Wherever she and the coaching staff went, they too represented the Lady Chargers. All I know is, I would have never acted or reacted with the media the way she did.

So, the next day, I went to practice early and stopped by her office. I told her what I had heard the night before and how it discouraged and saddened me. She seemed very shocked and surprised that I was mentioning these things. I went on to tell her that she was representing all of us and I would have never handled that situation the way she did. She seemed more amazed. Then she paused and finally asked me if I thought she owed the team an apology? (Honestly, I had not thought it all the way through, but that sounded good, so I told her yes.) She agreed and told me she would do it as soon as she came down for practice. I was shocked and I left her office headed to the gym.

Well…somewhere between me leaving her office and her making it to the gymnasium floor, she had some other thoughts! When she arrived, she seemed furious. She found every little thing wrong with my performance that day on the court and made me run laps or suicides all during practice. This happened the rest of the season. She also removed me off the starting line-up and many players begin to quit the team due to her bad attitude. She seemingly didn't care! She'd rather lose the rest of the season than to admit she was wrong. The Athletic Director met with me privately for lunch one day asking me what was going on and why wasn't I starting anymore. I told him everything. He told me not to worry and to not let it get to me. He told me not to quit the team.

Yet, it got to me every game! I'd sit on the bench game after game with tears welled up in my eyes desiring to play as I knew I could make a difference in the game. I recall once, my brother and his then girlfriend drove all the way from Florida to see me play and the only time I got to touch the ball was during warm-ups. My teammates told me I should quit night after night and that I should take my talent elsewhere. After all, the university next door, Alabama A & M's coach had shown interest. But I was determined to not quit simply because I felt this was the coach's entire motive. I'd cry at night, but I never let her see me cry. (I recall all the trips she made to my Junior College trying to convince me to sign with her team. And she even continued calling me even after I had signed with Georgia Southern.)

So part of me wondered was I being punished for breaking my commitment to the Georgia Southern coach. Yet the other part of me was sure that I was suffering all of this due to my need to speak up and confront wrong. ***We all must be willing to stand, even if we have to stand alone.***

Before I confronted her, we had a winning record and an awesome team filled with talent, one that could have won a championship that season. Afterwards, our team fell apart, players quit one behind another, and the season became very long and unbearable. In the end, we had a losing record. Yet I refused to quit!!! At the end of season, she called me into her office and told me she admired me. She told me she tried her best to break my spirit and cause me to quit; yet I stood. She applauded me and wished me the best. She then resigned. I went on to play another season under a new coach and eventually traveled overseas to play professionally.

So, know that some people would rather *lose* relationships, games, business deals, etc. all because they have *too much pride*. They'd rather allow themselves and everything around them to fall apart than to confess they are wrong. However, don't ever be too proud to say you are wrong. Life and common sense should tell us all that where there are two or more people involved in a relationship, each one will be guilty at some point for the breakdown and let downs that are sure to happen. *The only way to grow is to admit faults, let them go and move forward.*

So, I say to you, *SHOW UP, SPEAK UP and STAND UP!* No matter what environment you find yourself in. Even though fear is present, as it was in me the day I walked into her office, do it anyway! You will feel better afterwards knowing you stood up.

TESTIMONIALS

"Doc, many people have chosen to be a Motivational Speaker, but you've been *called* and *anointed* to be a speaker for you are destroying yokes. That's why you have the long lines outside of your classes an hour before you present. The anointing draws people. The reason I continue to come to your seminars because you have *never* presented it the same way, not even twice. You are no longer flying, you have gone into orbit now!" (Pastor Eddie Royal, Los Angeles, CA (who has heard "Do it **Afraid**!" over 10+ times))

"Because of the stories you shared, I'm stepping out of my comfort zone today. I realize now I'm not the only one who has so many fears. Thank you for being so transparent. Thank you for presenting the seminar twice today. I was too afraid to come sit in your seminar, so I dialed in from my desk. I'm so glad I did." (Justin at Port Hueneme, CA Naval Base)

"Of all the sessions I attended at BEST, your presentation is still resonating with me. I feel like it was a divine appointment and I was meant to be in your session. I find myself accepting new opportunities and going outside my comfort zone, because I'm doing it afraid." (Ledlyne H. Vazquez)

"Wow! Powerful messages! Keep it coming! Thanks for sharing your thoughts. **Close your eyes and look through your ears.**

There is a calling for you. Look, listen and follow. Your voice is heavenly music. I Love your voice!" (Brannon Knox, San Diego, CA)

"You are a blessing to so many people in so many different ways, continue to witness the goodness of his grace and favor over your life, tell your story and watch God do the rest. Dr. Stewart was here presenting 2015 B.I.G. NTI and all her seminars were standing room only and many were blessed as well as herself!" (Cheryl Peterson, Seattle, WA)

"May God continue to give you opportunities to "Press" and to "Do it Afraid." I am proud to know you and call you my friend." (Pastor Charles Bennafield, Stone Mountain, GA)

"I attended both of your awesome seminars! ("Do it Afraid!" and "It's Time to Press!") Thanks for sharing! What a blessing!" (Rirette Wilkerson)

"You are a cold glass of water in a very hot and dry desert. Your voice is so critically needed in this hour." (An elderly lady at 2015 BIG NTI)

"Val, you are a great inspiration to me. I always enjoy your words of encouragement, success and wisdom. Girl you are awesome. Keep up the good work!!" (Theresa Ward Sykes)

"When we make ourselves available to God trusting fully in Him, He will use us. You are testimony to that! So proud of your faith in God and trusting in

His will for all things! May you always go forth in His anointing! The harvest is plentiful, but the laborers are few. Thank you for being a laborer for Christ!" (Beth Sartor James, Destin, FL)

"I attended the first presentation at the BIG NTI. After your presentation I felt empowered to do more, not only for my job, but also for my community. Thanks again for sharing your story." (Phil)

"It is with esteemed pleasure to have had the opportunity to meet you, hear a powerful and encouraging speech (from the heart) as well as fellowship with you after the event...You were indeed a blessing to all of us." (Dr. Horne, D.C.)

"Your presence was a very important reason for the symposiums success and again we are so thankful." (Tony Dias, Hawaii)

"It was such a delight to meet you and become inspired by your presentation in San Diego a couple of weeks ago. It was a blessing to be there!!!!" (Richard Hamada, Hawaii)

"Your story is a powerful story and needs to be shared on a greater scale." (Minister Charlie Holley)

"It was so nice meeting you this weekend at the Women Who Pray event. Thank you for blessing us with your presence! I want you to know that this was truly a life changing experience for me - your positive words have encouraged me to see and seek God in every action that I take on my road to becoming a billionaire." (Danna K. Johnston, Seattle, Washington)

""Do it Afraid" and "Maximize your Potential" both presentations were excellent and you presented the material in a motivating style that allowed attendees to fully connect with you. Thank you for that." (R. Shawn Henderson)

"I wanted to let you know your seminar was OUTSTANDING!!! You will never know how much information I received from you. I believe I've been living my life for other people instead of myself. I'm a person who always wants to help; however, I have a very difficult time saying no and expressing my feelings. After listening to you, I've been re-thinking on how I'm going to live the rest of my life." (Lennetta Elias)

"Thank you so much. I tell you, I truly enjoyed your class; it has really motivated me in so many ways. It's exciting when you are motivated to push forward and to know that you "Can." May God continue blessing you; praise him for Motivational speakers as yourself. Thank you again for an eye-opener seminar/conference." (Yvonne Jennings)

"I was touched by both of your presentations at the National Training Institute - what a shining star that you bring to people lives. I enjoyed the training and your positive message. I would greatly appreciate both of your briefings. If ever in need of a speaker, I am going to spread the word of your attributes." (Charles Novell)

"I attended your seminar and purchased the "Do it Afraid" CD. I've played it over and over again and have even shared it with others. I stepped ought of my fears, applied and received a job I always wanted. I helped my daughter and neighbor step out of their fears as well, start businesses and other things using your methods. Your message has literally changed my life and I'm now speedily using your message to change other's lives that I come into contact with. (Will)

"This is your calling. I'm not telling you to go quit your engineering job on Monday morning, but I will say, you need to *find* a way to launch out and do this full time for you've been called to do this. I'm a Senior Executive Service (SES) in D.C. and have no reasons to change anything in the way I manage people, but after hearing you today, I'm going back and do some things differently." SES in D.C.

"Do it Afraid!"

Dr. Valerie Martin-Stewart

CPSIA information can be obtained
at www.ICGtesting.com
Printed in the USA
BVOW09s0323290917
496194BV00001B/1/P